RAMAYANA

for

CHILDREN

by

Neela Subramaniam

YOUNG KIDS PRESS

An imprint of Sura Books (Pvt) Ltd.

(An ISO 9001:2000 Certified Company)

Chennai • Ernakulam
Bengalooru • Thiruvananthapuram

Price: Rs.150.00

© PUBLISHERS

RAMAYANA FOR CHILDREN (ENGLISH)

By Neela Subramaniam

This Edition	:	June, 2009
Size	:	1/4 Demy
Pages	:	96
Illustrated by	:	V. Arumugam (Mayil)
Digitally Coloured, Layout & Designed by	:	Sura's Digital Studio

Price: Rs.150.00

ISBN: 81-7478-489-6

[NO ONE IS PERMITTED TO COPY OR TRANSLATE IN ANY OTHER LANGUAGE THE CONTENTS OF THIS BOOK OR PART THEREOF IN ANY FORM WITHOUT THE WRITTEN PERMISSION OF THE PUBLISHERS]

YOUNG KIDS PRESS

[An imprint of Sura Books (Pvt) Ltd.]

Head Office : 1620, 'J' Block, 16th Main Road, Anna Nagar, **Chennai - 600 040.**
Phones: 044-26162173, 26161099.

Branches :
- XXXII/2328, New Kalavath Road, Opp. to BSNL, Near Chennoth Glass, Palarivattom, **Ernakulam - 682 025.** Phones: 0484-3205797, 2535636
- TC 27/2162, Chirakulam Road, Statue, **Thiruvananthapuram - 695 001.** Phone : 0471-2570445.
- 3638/A, IVth Cross, Opp. to Malleswaram Railway Station, Gayathri Nagar, Back gate of Subramaniya Nagar, **Bengalooru - 560 021.** Phone: 080-23324950

Printed at S.S. Colour Impression Pvt Ltd. Chennai - 600 106 and Published by V.V.K.Subburaj for Young Kids Press [An imprint of Sura Books (Pvt) Ltd.] 1620, 'J' Block, 16th Main Road, Anna Nagar, Chennai - 600 040. Phones: 26162173, 26161099. Fax: (91) 44-26162173. e-mail: enquiry@surabooks.com; website: www.surabooks.com

CONTENTS

		Page
	Introduction	1
1.	In The Beginning	2
2.	The Birth Of Rama	4
3.	The Sons Of Dasaratha	8
4.	Taataka's End	10
5.	At Viswamitra's Ashram	12
6.	Mithila	13
7.	Ahalya	14
8.	Rama Wins Sita's Hand	15
9.	King Dasaratha's Wish	19
10.	Manthara Poisons Kaikeyi's Mind	20
11.	Kaikeyi Demands Her Boons	22
12.	King Dasaratha's Anguish	23
13.	Rama Leaves Ayodhya	25
14.	Rama Meets Guha	27
15.	In Ayodhya	29
16.	Bharata's Home-coming	31
17.	Rama Journeys On	33
18.	Bharata Meets Rama	34
19.	Rama To The Rescue	37
20.	Enter Surpanakha	38
21.	Rama Slays The Rakshasa Hordes	40
22.	The Golden Deer	42
23.	Ravana Abducts Sita	44
24.	Brave Jataayu	45
25.	Rama's Grief	46
26.	Kabandha's Advice	47
27.	Rama Meets Hanuman	48
28.	Sugriva's Sad Story	49
29.	Rama Vows To Help Sugriva	50
30.	Sugriva's Sudden Doubt	51

		Page
31.	Rama Slays Vali	52
32.	Sugriva Is Reminded Of His Promise	54
33.	The Search For Sita Begins	55
34.	Hanuman Travels Southward	57
35.	Sampaati's Tale	58
36.	Hanuman Crosses The Ocean	60
37.	Hanuman In Lanka	61
38.	Sita In The Asoka Vana	63
39.	Ravana Warns Sita	63
40.	Hanuman Gives Rama's Ring To Sita	65
41.	Lanka On Fire	68
42.	Hanuman's Happy Tidings To Rama	72
43.	Rumblings In Lanka	73
44.	Vibheeshana Surrenders	74
45.	Building The Bridge To Lanka	76
46.	Angada Is Sent As Messenger	77
47.	Ravana's Tactics	78
48.	The War Begins	79
49.	Ravana Humbled	82
50.	Kumbakarna Is Roused	83
51.	The Death Of Ravana	87
52.	Sita's Ordeal By Fire	89
53.	Rama Meets Bharata	90

Ramayana for Children

Introduction

No Indian child needs any introduction to the stories of RAMA and KRISHNA. The stories we hear at our mothers' knees remain with us forever. Indeed, it is not wrong to say that our two great epics, "THE RAMAYANA" and "THE MAHABHARATA" have a timeless quality. One can never tire of reading them again and again, learning new lessons from them every time.

The story of RAMA is the story of an ideal son, an ideal brother, an ideal husband, an ideal friend and an ideal King. So, RAMA is known and revered in India as "MARYADA PURUSHOTTAMA RAMA."

The "RAMAYANA" is respected not only in different parts of India, but is much treasured in many South-East Asian countries. This great epic lends itself readily to different forms of artistic expression - in poetry, in prose, in music, in art, in dance and in drama.

May all readers of "RAMAYANA FOR CHILDREN" published by SURA BOOKS (Pvt) LTD., absorb the sterling qualities of LORD RAMACHANDRA of Ayodhya and experience the same bliss the writer derived when retelling the great epic.

1. In The Beginning

The story of "THE RAMAYANA" is lost in the mists of time and goes back many hundreds of years. It was first handed down by word of mouth for generations. Let us take a look at the beginning...

One day, the Divine Sage, Narada, visited Valmiki's ashrama beside the flowing Tamasa river.

"Welcome, O great Narada!" Valmiki spread a mat of "kusa" grass and offered the traditional flowers, fruits and water. "Please can you help me to find the answer to a question which has been troubling me for a long time?"

The Divine Sage smiled to himself as he knew through his supernatural powers, what Valmiki wanted to know.

"O Valmiki! Ask me and I will certainly tell you!" he said in reply.

"O Sage Narada! Who among the great heroes of this world is outstanding in virtue and wisdom?" asked Valmiki.

"The answer to that question is very easy! Ramachandra, who belongs to the Solar Dynasty, and is the King of Ayodhya, is the greatest hero!" said Sage Narada.

"Please can you tell me why?" asked Valmiki.

He listened with great interest while Sage Narada told him in detail the story of Rama. Even after the Sage Narada had left, Valmiki constantly thought of Rama all day.

As Valmiki went to offer his morning prayers in the Tamasa river, he saw two "krauncha" birds playing lovingly. Suddenly an arrow hit the male bird and it fell to the ground while its mate, the female, chirped piteously.

Valmiki's heart melted with pity at the sight and he flew into a great rage. He cursed the hunter, "O hunter! You have killed an innocent playful bird; so, you will wander homeless for long!"

As Valmiki meditated deeply, he received a radiant vision of Lord Brahma, the Creator.

"O Valmiki! Your pity for the dead bird has found expression in a beautiful verse. In the same form, you will

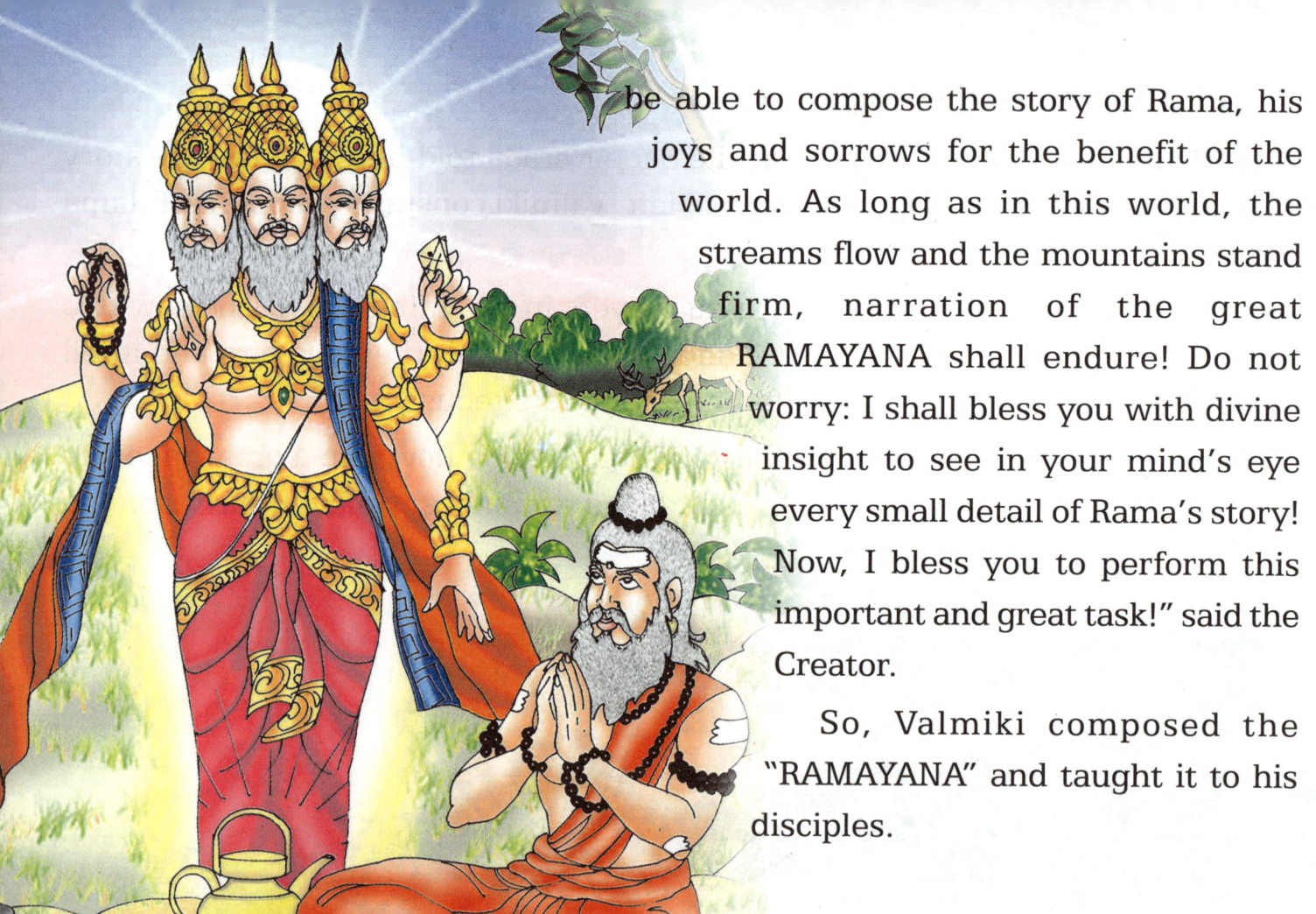

be able to compose the story of Rama, his joys and sorrows for the benefit of the world. As long as in this world, the streams flow and the mountains stand firm, narration of the great RAMAYANA shall endure! Do not worry: I shall bless you with divine insight to see in your mind's eye every small detail of Rama's story! Now, I bless you to perform this important and great task!" said the Creator.

So, Valmiki composed the "RAMAYANA" and taught it to his disciples.

2. The Birth of Rama

The great kingdom of Kosala lay to the north of the mighty river Ganga. Its capital, Ayodhya (which means that which cannot be conquered) was situated beside the flowing Sarayu river.

Ayodhya was a beautiful, well-planned city, protected by its strong forts and moats. The ruler of Kosala was **King Dasaratha** of the Solar Dynasty. He was a great King who cared deeply for the welfare of his subjects. The people of Kosala were extremely happy under Dasaratha's rule and lived contented lives.

King Dasaratha had three wives - **Kausalya, Sumitra** and **Kaikeyi**. Though Dasaratha loved all his wives dearly, he was specially fond of his youngest queen, **Kaikeyi**. But in the midst of their happiness, was a deep sorrow - they had no sons.

"I shall seek the advice of Sage Vasishta and my ministers", King Dasaratha decided and called a conference.

"O great Vasishta! I am worried that there will be no son to inherit my throne. What can I do? Please give me your advice!" said King Dasaratha.

"O King! We would all advise you to perform a 'yaaga' for progeny to continue your illustrious line!" said Sage Vasishta.

"Please tell me, who will conduct this 'yaaga'?" asked King Dasaratha.

"The great Sage Rishyashringa should be brought to Ayodhya for the 'yaaga'", Sage Vasishta replied.

So, preparations for the "yaaga" began in Ayodhya.

At that very time, all the Devas held a conference in Swargaloka.

"The rakshasa Ravana is growing more powerful with the passing of each day and is a menace not only to us, Devas, but to all mankind as well! We must ask Lord Brahma for help!"

They all went to Satyaloka to see the Creator.

"O Lord Brahma! Please can you save us from the wicked rakshasa Ravana?" they prayed with folded hands.

"O Devas! I am totally helpless in this regard as Ravana performed severe 'tapas' to obtain a boon from me which would protect him from Devas, Gandharvas and Asuras", said Brahma. He thought for a moment and went on, "but in his supreme arrogance, Ravana did not ask for protection from mankind! So, we must ask Lord Vishnu to help us!"

Lord Brahma and the Devas went to Vaikuntham to see Lord Vishnu. They told him about the rakshasa Ravana and the boon he had obtained from Brahma, as well as the omission.

"Please help us somehow!" they begged.

Vishnu smiled at them.

"Cast away your fears at once! The good King Dasaratha is performing a 'yaaga' for sons now. I will be born as his son, Rama, and will slay the rakshasa Ravana."

The Devas rejoiced greatly and went away.

The Sage Rishyashringa poured sacrificial "ghee" into the fire while the other sages chanted Vedic "mantras". Towards the end of the "yaaga", the flames shot up and a celestial form emerged from the fire, holding a golden bowl in his hand. It was the God of Fire, Agni Deva.

"O King Dasaratha! The Devas are pleased with you and have decided to answer your prayers by blessing you with sons. Ask your wives to drink this special 'payasam' in this bowl they have sent", Agni Deva said and handed the bowl to King Dasaratha.

Dasaratha accepted the bowl with great joy. He asked his eldest Queen, Kausalya, to drink half of the "payasam". He gave half of what remained to Sumitra and a part of what was left to Kaikeyi. He asked Sumitra to drink the remaining "payasam" in the golden bowl.

Soon four sons were born to the Queens of King Dasaratha. Kausalya gave birth to Rama (who was the incarnation of Vishnu), Bharata was born to Kaikeyi, Sumitra became the mother of the twins, Lakshmana and Shatrughna (as she had partaken of the divine "payasam" two times).

All Ayodhya rejoiced with King Dasaratha and his Queens. The royal palace came alive with the sound of childish laughter and play. King Dasaratha loved all his four sons, but was specially fond of Rama, who was the eldest. Rama was the apple of his eye and he could not bear to be apart from him for even a short time!

3. The Sons of Dasaratha

One day, King Dasaratha was discussing some state matters with Sage Vasishta and other ministers at court when a messenger arrived with important news.

"The famous Sage, Viswamitra, is coming to see you, O King!" the messenger bowed and said.

King Dasaratha was overjoyed to hear this. He rose from his throne and came to meet the great Sage.

"Welcome O great one! I am very fortunate to receive you as my guest. Is there anything which I can do for you? Command me and I shall obey at once!" said King Dasaratha.

"O King! I am greatly pleased to hear your gracious words. You have agreed to help me even before I asked you! As you belong to the great Ishvaku Dynasty, I know that you will keep your word!" exclaimed Viswamitra.

"Please tell me what I can do for you!" repeated King Dasaratha.

"Then listen, O King Dasaratha!" Viswamitra began. "I am performing a great sacrifice. But two rakshasas, **Mareecha** and **Subahu** defile the sacred fire by throwing human flesh and blood. I could curse them but it would interrupt my sacrifice. So, please send Rama with me to slay the rakshasas. I will keep him for about ten days and then send him back to Ayodhya!"

King Dasaratha was unprepared to hear this and was very shocked too.

"O Sage Viswamitra! How can I send a young boy like Rama to face fierce rakshasas!? Rama is my very life and I will die if anything happens to him! I will send my army to protect you and your sacrifice. Please agree to this!" he cried.

Viswamitra became very angry.

"O King Dasaratha! It does not become of a ruler of the illustrious Ishvaku line to go back on his word as you have just done. Tell me, is this your final word...that you will not send Rama with me?" his eyes flashed.

Sage Vasishta came forward.

"O King Dasaratha! You need not fear about sending Rama to kill the rakshasas. Lakshmana can go with Rama. Viswamitra will protect them from any danger. Remember, O King, that Viswamitra was a great warrior and is skilled in the use of divine weapons, who performed severe 'tapas' to attain the exalted position of **'Brahma Rishi'!**" he said soothingly.

King Dasaratha was encouraged by Sage Vasishta's wise advice. So, he sent for Rama and Lakshmana.

"My sons, go with the great Viswamitra and help him to perform his sacrifice. Obey him all the time as he knows what is best for you. May you all be successful!" Dasaratha blessed his sons and sent them forth.

4. Taataka's End

Rama and Lakshmana shouldered their great bows and walked proudly on either side of Sage Viswamitra as he led them to the forest. They presented a resplendent picture of handsome youth beside mature wisdom.

As they journeyed along, Viswamitra pointed out places of interest and told the two Princes why the places were memorable. Soon they crossed the Ganga and entered the Dandaka Forest.

The whole forest was a wilderness and there was no sight of humans. Only wild animals lived there apart from sages who sought seclusion for "tapas". Rama asked why this was so.

"The Dandaka forest is inhabited by a rakshasi called Taataka and her son Mareecha. It was a beautiful forest, alive with flowering trees, wild animals and birds. But no one enters the Dandaka forest now out of fear of Taataka and Mareecha. Taataka is very hideous and has the strength of a thousand elephants. She and her son have been harassing the sages here. So, I want you to kill Taataka and restore Dandaka to its former beauty!" explained Viswamitra.

"Our father has told us to obey you!" said Rama and twanged the string of his great bow loudly.

The sound reached the ears of Taataka who was in her cave. She roared angrily and came out shouting, "Who dares to disturb me?"

Taataka saw Rama and Lakshmana and laughed, "What! Have you young lads come to fight with me? HA! HA!! HAA!!!"

A fierce battle began between Rama and Lakshmana on one side and Taataka on the other.

Rama was quite surprised to find that Taataka was strong for a woman.

"Rama! Remember that rakshasas and rakshasis grow stronger at night. The Sun is about to set. So, kill Taataka at once without delay and do not hesitate because she is a woman!" warned Viswamitra.

So, Rama shot an arrow which pierced Taataka's chest. She fell down lifeless and the whole place shook with the impact.

Dandaka forest regained its lost beauty. The sages thanked Rama and Lakshmana for ridding them of the rakshasi.

5. At Viswamitra's Ashram

Viswamitra was delighted with Rama's skill in archery.

"I shall teach you how to use other weapons effectively. You can impart the knowledge to Lakshmana", he said and proceeded to train them in the use of many weapons he had obtained after performing "tapas".

The three of them continued the journey to Sage Viswamitra's ashrama. Soon they neared a beautiful forest with many flowering plants and trees on a hill slope.

"Is that your ashrama there?" Rama pointed. "What a lovely place!"

"Yes. It is called Siddhashrama", Viswamitra replied.

They were all greeted by his many disciples who were ready to participate in the "yaaga", and were happy that Rama would be there to help them against the rakshasas.

Rama and Lakshmana stood guard with bows in their hands while Sage Viswamitra began his "yaaga". Things went smoothly for the first few days. Then, on the last day of the "yaaga", there was a loud another roar from above.

Rama and Lakshmana looked up and saw hordes of rakshasas led by Mareecha and Subahu flying over the area. They threw bits of flesh and blood into the sacrificial fire, thereby polluting it.

Rama shot a divine weapon he had learnt from Viswamitra. It did not kill Mareecha, but the force of the weapon hurled Mareecha hundreds of miles away into the sea. Subahu was killed by a flaming weapon flung at him by Rama.

Viswamitra and all his disciples were overjoyed that they could conclude the "yaaga" in peace, without the distraction and pollution caused by the rakshasas.

Through his supernatural powers, Viswamitra was aware of the purpose of Rama's birth. He knew that he still had another important task to perform in this regard.

"All of us will be going to the city of Mithila in the kingdom of Videha, ruled by the wise **King Janaka.** He is performing a great sacrifice and we wish to be present. Besides, he has a great bow of Siva, in his palace. Accompany us and you will see the bow!" said Viswamitra.

Rama and Lakshmana agreed at once to go with Viswamitra and his disciples to Mithila.

6. Mithila

The vast kingdom of Videha, whose capital was **Mithila,** was ruled by King Janaka. He was a very wise and good King, like Dasaratha. The two of them were good friends too.

Once King Janaka was ploughing the field before the start of a "yaaga". He found a beautiful baby girl lying among the furrows. As King Janaka was childless, he looked upon the baby girl as Mother Earth's gift to him.

"What a wonderful treasure you have found! We shall bring her up as our own daughter and call her **Sita** as she was found in the furrow at the 'yaaga' site!" exclaimed his happy Queen. The royal pair did not know that the beautiful child was really the Goddess Lakshmi reborn as a human being.

Sita grew up to be a very beautiful maiden, educated, talented and charming. As she reached marriageable age, King Janaka and his Queen decided that they could give her in marriage only to a man who was truly worthy in every respect.

King Janaka had in his possession a great bow given to him by Lord Siva. It was very big and so heavy that an ordinary man would not be able to lift it. Only an outstanding man could do so.

So, King Janaka proclaimed throughout his kingdom that a great "yaaga" would first be held, followed by a "swayamvara" for Sita's hand.

Viswamitra, who knew who Sita was, decided to take Rama to Mithila and so unite the Divine Couple.

7. Ahalya

On the way to Mithila, Rama saw a beautiful ashrama. It looked deserted.

"O great Sage Viswamitra! To whom does this ashrama belong? Why is it looking so desolate? Does no one live here?" Rama asked.

"This ashrama is under a curse; that is why it looks desolate. The great Sage Gautama lived here happily with his beautiful wife, Ahalya", said Viswamitra.

"What happened?" asked Rama and Lakshmana.

"One day, Indra, the King of the Devas happened to pass by. He saw Ahalya and fell in love with her. Indra desired Ahalya deeply and decided to play a trick on the Sage and his wife.

"'I am going to the river nearby and will not be back for some time, stay here safely!' Sage Gautama said to his wife, Ahalya, one morning.

"Indra waited till Gautama had gone some distance away. Then he changed his appearance to look exactly like Sage Gautama and went to the ashrama.

"Ahalya was surprised to see her husband back so soon. Indra, disguised as Gautama, took advantage of her.

"The real Sage Gautama returned to the ashrama suddenly. He saw his wife with the imposter and became very angry.

"'You both have sinned greatly! For this you shall be cursed; Ahalya, to become a stone till Ramachandra of Ayodhya comes this way and touches you with his feet!' Gautama remarked as he went away to do penance.

At once ahalya was turned into stone to wait for Rama to come to the place.

"This is the story of Ahalya and Sage Gautama. Rama, only you can redeem Ahalya from the curse. Do release her quickly!" said Viswamitra.

Rama gently placed his foot on the stone. And lo! At the touch of Rama's foot, the stone was transformed into a beautiful woman. It was Ahalya, cleansed of her sin. Sage Gautama returned from the Himalayas where he had gone to do "tapas", at that very moment.

"O Ahalya! You have been purified by Rama's touch, so, I accept you as my wife once more!" he said to her.

Rama was happy that he could help Ahalya. Viswamitra then led the other sages, his disciples and the two princes of Ayodhya on to the city of Mithila.

8. Rama Wins Sita's Hand

"Look, Rama, preparations for the great 'yaaga' to be performed by King Janaka are nearly complete. Let us go and pay our respects to the King!" Viswamitra said and took the princes to Janaka's court.

Messengers informed King Janaka about the arrival of Sage Viswamitra, in Mithila. He was very glad to hear this and personally went to receive Viswamitra.

"O great Sage! I am indeed very fortunate that you have come to Mithila to participate in the 'yaaga'. I see that two Royal Princes have accompanied you here. Who are they?" he asked.

"O King Janaka! These are Rama and Lakshmana, the sons of King Dasaratha of Ayodhya. They are accomplished warriors. I would like Rama to test the great bow of Siva which you have!" replied Viswamitra.

"I will be very happy if Rama can string the bow. After the 'yaaga' is over, a 'swayamvara' is to be held. Many princely suitors have gathered here to test Siva's bow.

If anyone can string it successfully, he shall marry my daughter, Sita!" said King Janaka.

Viswamitra and the other sages all participated in the "yaaga". When it was over, they assembled to King Janaka's court to see Sita's "swayamvara".

Many strong Kings and Princes were seated in the great hall. Sita stood by the King and Queen with the rose garland in her hand. Her eyes fell on Rama who was sitting beside Sage Viswamitra. Rama too looked at Sita that very moment and the two of them were instantly attracted to each other.

Sita looked on as each suitor including Ravana tested Siva's bow. She was secretly pleased when none of them could even lift the bow.

All eyes were on Rama as he stepped towards the great bow, after bowing to King Janaka and Sage Viswamitra. He closed his eyes reverently and bowed to Siva mentally before he even touched the bow.

To the utter astonishment of all present, Rama lifted the bow and balanced it against his big toe to string it. There was a loud thunderous clap as the bow snapped into two.

Sita was very happy that Rama has succeeded and garlanded Rama. King Janaka was overjoyed. He has been deeply impressed by Rama and now felt that Rama would be worthy of Sita in every respect.

"It gives me great pleasure to announce that I will give my daughter, Sita, in marriage to Rama, Prince of Ayodhya!" He announced in the assembled court which broke out into loud applause.

"O King Janaka, send your swiftest messengers at once to King Dasaratha at Ayodhya to convey the glad tidings and ask him to come at once for the marriage celebrations!" said Sage Viswamitra.

King Janaka's messengers set out immediately.

"Salutations to the great King Dasaratha from King Janaka of Videha! King Janaka has asked us to inform you that Prince Rama has successfully strung - and even broken - Siva's bow, a condition which the King made, in order to win the Princess Sita's hand. King Janaka invites you all to bless the couple at this marriage and eagerly waits for your arrival in Mithila", said the messengers.

King Dasaratha, who had been secretly very anxious after sending Rama with Viswamitra, despite Sage Vasishta's advice and encouragement, was delighted to hear about Rama's new conquest! He set out at once with a large entourage for

Mithila. King Janaka received them all with full honours and befitting the members of the bridegroom's party.

At the very time Rama was married to Sita, Lakshmana was married to Sita's sister, Urmila. Bharata and Shatrughna too were married to Sita's cousins (King Janaka's nieces), Mandavi and Srutakirti.

"What a wonderful couple Rama and Sita make!", Sage Viswamitra smiled to himself when he heard everyone saying. He knew that they were the Divine Couple, Vishnu and Lakshmi, born on earth for the benefit of mankind.

The marriage celebrations went on for days as King Janaka was desirous to make it truly grand. Soon after the celebrations came to an end, Sage Viswamitra returned to his ashrama, King Dasaratha, his sons and their wives, and all who had gone to Mithila for the marriage, set out on the return journey to Ayodhya.

Their progress was quite smooth till a great storm broke out, with great claps of thunder.

"Do not worry, O King Dasaratha! Nothing can harm us!" Sage Vasishta said to an anxious King.

All of a sudden, the radiant figure of Parasurama, stood before them all.

"O Rama! I have just heard that you broke Siva's bow at Mithila. I want to challenge you! Here is my bow which was given to Vishnu. Let me see if you can string it with the same ease!" said Parasurama in a loud voice which sounded like thunder.

"O Parasurama! We know that you are a Brahmin who vowed to slay all Kshatriya Kings to avenge your father's death at the hands of a Kshatriya King. Please spare Rama! What harm has he done to you?" begged King Dasaratha in trembling tones as he was terrified by the angry-looking Parasurama.

Parasurama ignored him and repeated his challenge to Rama.

Rama smiled and took the bow from Parasurama. He strung it effortlessly and fitted an arrow and looked at Parasurama.

"Tell me, O great Parasurama, where should I aim this arrow?" Rama asked gently with a smile.

At once Parasurama realised that Rama was no ordinary being, but Lord Vishnu himself!

"I have just realised who you are. You have completely removed my pride. I shall go back to the Himalayas to continue with my 'tapas'!" Parasurama said in a mild tone and went away.

King Dasaratha was very relieved. The huge party reached Ayodhya where the people celebrated the marriage of their beloved Prince Rama with great joy.

9. King Dasaratha's Wish

Rama and Sita lived happily in Ayodhya for over a decade. Sita was the ideal daughter-in-law and greatly loved not only by all the Queens, but by the people too.

King Dasaratha's happiness knew no bounds. As he was getting old, he had one desire left - to crown Rama as his successor to the throne. He called a meeting at court and consulted Sage Vasishta and his other ministers.

"I have one wish and I hope that you all will agree with my proposal. As I am getting old, I wish to crown Rama as King of Ayodhya. What do you all say?" he asked.

"O King! Everyone in the kingdom loves Rama dearly for his sterling qualities. He will be the ideal choice to ascend the throne!" Sage Vasishta applauded. The same sentiment was expressed by all the other ministers too.

"I am very happy that you all agree with me!" exclaimed King Dasaratha.

"O King! This is an auspicious time for the coronation. Please start preparations rightaway!" said Sage Vasishta.

"It is a pity that Bharata and Shatrughna have gone to Kekaya and will not be present!" said Dasaratha.

When Queen Kausalya heard the news, she was extremely happy.

"Rama deserves the honour!" Sumitra said.

Dasaratha sent for Rama.

"Rama, I am getting on in years. I wish to anoint you as my successor to the throne", he said.

"I shall be happy to do whatever you decide!" Rama said and left the King's apartment to inform Sita.

Dasaratha consulted his advisers and called for Rama again.

"Please begin preparations for your coronation right now. We have decided to hold the ceremony as quickly as possible!" King Dasaratha instructed.

Rama bowed and said, "I shall be pleased to obey you!"

10. Manthara Poisons Kaikeyi's Mind

When King Dasaratha had married Kaikeyi, the Princess of Kekaya, she had brought with her to Ayodhya, a hunchbacked companion named Manthara. Manthara was disturbed when she saw the festive preparations going on. She was very upset when she learned the reason for the preparations.

She ran as fast as she could to Kaikeyi's royal apartment. Kaikeyi was lying on her couch.

"Rise, O foolish Kaikeyi! Do you know what is going to happen soon?" she screamed angrily.

"What?" Kaikeyi smiled at her.

"The King Dasaratha has planned to crown Rama as his successor to the throne!" Manthara informed her.

Kaikeyi arose from her couch and hugged Manthara.

"What wonderful news you have given me! I love Rama as my own son and he will be an ideal ruler! Here, take this necklace!" Kaikeyi took off her precious necklace and gave it to Manthara as a reward for bringing good news. But Manthara flung it aside angrily.

"Do not be so confident and think of your own position! You always tell me that the King loves you best, but it is Kausalya's son, Rama, who is going to be crowned, not your own son, Bharata! It will be a sad day for you if Rama is crowned. He is the son of Kausalya. You will have to bow humbly to Rama and to Kausalya

too. Think of it! The King has cleverly chosen a time when your son, Bharata, is absent! From now, you will have to be second to Kausalya!" Manthara said.

Kaikeyi thought over the matter and began to be scared.

"O Manthara! What shall I do? Kausalya will certainly expect me to be humble if her son is crowned!" Kaikeyi looked worried. Her heart, which had been pure and full of love for Rama, now began turning against Rama whom she had regarded as her own son.

"Listen to me! I will help you so that your own son is crowned instead of Rama! Remember that the King promised you two boons, some time back when you saved his life on the battlefield?" Manthara realised that Kaikeyi would now listen to her words and was very pleased.

"Yes! But how can it prevent Rama's coronation?" Kaikeyi was puzzled.

"Let me explain... with the first boon, ask that Bharata should be crowned instead of Rama. Your second demand should be that Rama must be exiled to the forest for fourteen years", Manthara instructed Kaikeyi. "Listen to me - first cast away all your jewellery carelessly and dress in a torn garment. Lie down on the floor and refuse to talk to the King when he comes to see you. The King will try to change your mind. But be firm. Ask for Bharata to be crowned and Rama to be exiled to the forest!"

"All right, Manthara! I shall do exactly as you say!" Kaikeyi agreed, falling into Manthara's evil trap.

11. Kaikeyi Demands Her Boons

After a busy day of his many meetings with Sage Vasishta, Rama, his ministers and Queen Kausalya, King Dasaratha felt tired and decided to relax with his favourite Queen, Kaikeyi. He went to her royal apartment.

The King was surprised to see her jewels scattered on the floor. He was even more upset to see her lying, clad in an old garment, on the bare floor.

"Who has annoyed you, my dearest? Tell me and I shall punish him at once!" he said as he sat down beside her.

When Kaikeyi did not reply, Dasaratha repeated his question and promised to do whatever she wanted.

Kaikeyi sat up and said," Do you promise to do whatever I say?"

"Certainly, my dear. I swear on the head of Rama that I will obey you!" Dasaratha was glad that Kaikeyi was talking to him.

"Remember, O King, that long ago, I had saved your life on the battlefield. In gratitude, you had offered me two boons. I told you that I would ask for them later", Kaikeyi began.

"Yes, I shall certainly give you your two boons", said Dasaratha.

"Then, my first request is that you should crown Bharata instead of Rama. My second boon is that you should exile Rama to the forest to live like an ascetic for fourteen years", Kaikeyi said.

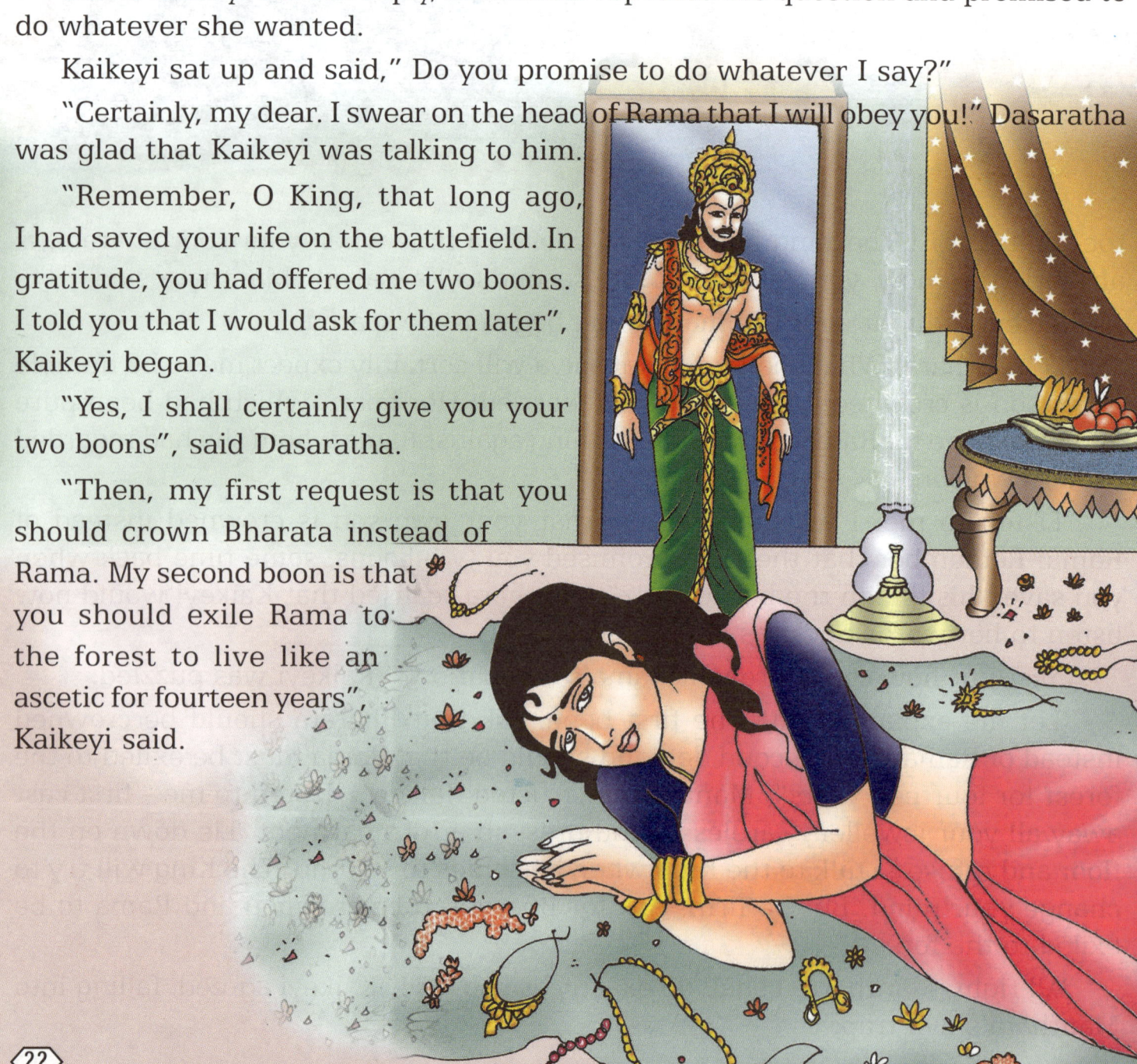

12. King Dasaratha's Anguish

King Dasaratha could not believe his ears. "Kaikeyi! What are you asking for? Have you not told me countless times that Rama is as dear to you as your own son?" he cried.

When Kaikeyi did not answer, Dasaratha went on, "No, Kaikeyi, I refuse to believe your cruel words! Someone has been poisoning your mind! What harm has Rama ever done to you that you should punish him thus?"

Kaikeyi laughed scornfully and said, "O King! It behoves a ruler of the Solar Dynasty to keep his word. You promised me two boons and I want them now. Crown Bharata and banish Rama to the forest for fourteen years!"

"I refuse to speak such unkind words to Rama!" Dasaratha groaned.

"Then I shall do it for you!" Kaikeyi remarked and summoned Dasaratha's minister Sumanthra. "O Sumanthra! Go at once and send Rama here! The King wishes to speak to him!"

Rama came at once to Kaikeyi's apartment. Dasaratha saw his beloved son and cried, "O Rama!"

Rama looked at Kaikeyi with concern and asked, "Mother, why is father upset, is he angry with me?"

Kaikeyi saw that Dasaratha was unwilling to talk. So, she took matters into her own hand.

"Your father once gave me two boons and I have asked for them now. He does not know how to tell you, so I shall do it for him! I want Bharata to be crowned instead of you, in the first place. Then I want you to go in exile to the forest for fourteen years and lead the life of an ascetic", she said.

"Oh, is that all? I will be very glad if my dear brother, Bharata is crowned. What is kingship to me if it can help my father to keep his promise? And, I will gladly go to live in the forest. Please tell father not to be so upset. I shall take leave of my mother before leaving for the forest!" Rama spoke calmly, without a trace of indignation in his voice.

Queen Kausalya was performing a special puja for Rama. Sita was with her. Also present were Sumitra and Lakshmana. Rama entered the room.

"Mother, please give me your blessings! I am proceeding to the forest to fulfil my father's promise made to mother Kaikeyi", Rama bowed to his own mother.

"But you are going to be crowned to ascend the throne!" Kausalya exclaimed with surprise.

"No, Mother, you are wrong! Bharata, my beloved brother, is to be crowned instead. I will go to live in the forest for fourteen years. Please give me your blessings! Sita, please take care of my mother while I am gone!" Rama said.

"My Lord, I shall accompany you to the forest", Sita announced calmly.

"You are a Princess so you are used to a comfortable existence. Life in the forest will be very hard. You will have to eat fruits, roots and berries, lie on the hard ground and protect yourself constantly from sudden attacks by wild animals in the forest!" Rama tried to dissuade Sita.

"No, my Lord, a wife's place is beside her husband both in joy and sorrow. So I have decided to go with you and share your difficulties. Besides, I know that you will protect me from any danger!" Sita said firmly.

"I too shall go with you, brother, to be of help in protecting you and serving you in any way I can. What is life here in ayodhya without you?" Lakshmana said.

"O son Lakshmana, go with my blessings with Rama and Sita and come back safely after the exile period of fourteen years!" Sumitra said and looked at Kausalya. "Do not worry, sister, my brave son loves Rama more than his own life and will look after both him and Sita!"

Rama, Sita and Lakshmana gave away all their possessions and dressed in austere ascetic garb. Then they went on foot to Kaikeyi's apartment to take leave of the King.

People who had gathered in happy anticipation of the coronation of their beloved Rama, were stunned to see their simple appearance and wondered what was happening. Why were they walking barefoot? they asked each other.

Rama entered Kaikeyi's apartments accompanied by Sita. News about Kaikeyi's boons and Rama's exile to the forest soon spread like wildfire throughout the city. People wept openly and cursed Kaikeyi for her hard-heartedness. What harm had Rama done to her, they asked.

13. Rama Leaves Ayodhya

Rama, Sita and Lakshmana entered Kaikeyi's royal apartment. King Dasaratha raised his head and saw with agony, his beloved son, Rama, clad in ascetic apparel. He cried broken-heartedly, "O Rama! Forgive me for the great wrong I have done to you!"

"Father, you have not done any wrong. We have come to take leave. Sita and Lakshmana have decided to go to the forest. Do not grieve, father, but comfort my mother in her sorrow. Let Bharata be crowned instead, and be happy. The fourteen years of my exile will pass very soon and I will be back in Ayodhya safely!" Rama said gently, his face betraying no emotion.

"I will ask Sumanthra to make arrangements so that your exile in the forest befits the status of a prince!" Dasaratha said in a low voice.

"What a fine way to live in exile! Do you want Bharata to rule over an empty kingdom?" Kaikeyi asked angrily.

"No, Father, I wish to lead the simple life of an ascetic! Please agree and let me go!" Rama said.

Dasaratha felt defeated.

"All right! But even Kaikeyi will not object if I order Sumanthra to take you all in the chariot to the border of the kingdom!" King Dasaratha said.

Kaikeyi did not say anything as she has obtained her boons.

Rama, Sita and Lakshmana left the palace of the weeping King and the gloating Kaikeyi.

King Dasaratha ran after the chariot carrying Rama, Sita and Lakshmana. Queen Kausalya and Queen Sumitra too followed the chariot. The people of Ayodhya ran behind the chariot, wanting to catch a last glimpse of Rama, Sita and Lakshmana, though many of them wanted to live in the forest with the exiles.

"O Rama! If you leave me, life will depart from this body of mine!" Dasaratha wept.

King Dasaratha stared at the chariot till it disappeared from sight and fell down unconscious. When he recovered, he looked at Kaikeyi with deep dislike and asked her if she was happy at last.

"I do not wish to stay with you a minute longer! Take me at once to Kausalya's apartment!" he ordered.

14. Rama Meets Guha

As the chariot carrying Rama, Sita and Lakshmana moved to the outskirts of the city, the people swarmed behind it. They loudly cursed Kaikeyi again and even said that Bharata would rule over an empty city.

Rama stopped the chariot and told the people to look upon Bharata with the same love they showered on him ... that Bharata was unaware of his mother's boons.

"Bharata will be your King and you must obey him. Go back to your houses now!" Rama said.

Many people shouted that they too would leave Ayodhya and spend their lives with Rama. For them Ayodhya was the place where Rama was!

Rama heard this and asked Sumanthra to drive the chariot faster, but still the people chased it. The chariot finally reached the bank of the flowing Tamasa river. Rama looked back and saw that the people had followed him.

Rama decided to spend the night on the bank of the river and asked Sumanthra to unharness the horses from the chariot. The people saw this and thinking that Rama would stay in the place, went to rest.

Unknown to them, some hours later, Rama awoke and whispered to Sita, Lakshmana and Sumanthra, "Let us leave quickly. The people are still tired and are fast asleep. We shall go away before anyone sees us. O' Sumanthra! Harness the horses to the chariot!"

Rama, Sita and Lakshmana went in the chariot.

When the people awoke the next morning, they found the chariot gone and no sign of Rama, Sita and Lakshmana. Disappointed, they all returned to their homes in Ayodhya.

In the meanwhile, the chariot with Rama, Sita and Lakshmana reached the banks of the Ganga. The three of them got down when Sumanthra stopped the chariot.

"We shall spend the night here on the bank of the holy Ganga and cross the river tomorrow morning", said Rama.

As they all rested beneath a tree, the hunter chieftain of the region, Guha, came up. He had heard about the happenings in Ayodhya. Guha folded his hands and requested Rama to stay with him during the 14 years of his exile, and that Sita would be looked after comfortably too.

Rama embraced Guha and said," O Guha! I know how much you love me! But it would not be fulfilling mother Kaikeyi's wish that I should lead the life of an

ascetic if I stay with you and enjoy some comforts. No, I cannot accept your hospitality. But I will be grateful if you can arrange a boat for us to cross the Ganga tomorrow morning!"

While Rama and Sita slept on a bed of grass which Lakshmana made for them, he himself remained awake.

"O Lakshmana! Go and rest! Sumanthra and I will stay awake to protect you!" Guha said.

"No, Guha! How can I sleep while my beloved brother and his wife have to lie on the hard ground?" Lakshmana asked with tears in his eyes.

Lakshmana, Sumanthra and Guha sat some distance away and spent the whole night talking.

The next morning, Guha told Rama that a large boat had been readied for them to cross the Ganga. Rama looked at Sumanthra's sad face and said consolingly, "O Sumanthra! The period of my exile has begun. Go back to Ayodhya and look after my aged father and my sorrowing mother. They need your support now!"

Rama, Sita and Lakshmana got into the boat. Guha ordered the boatman to row it across the Ganga. He stood with Sumanthra and watched as the boat sped over the water and carried Rama, Sita and Lakshmana away.

15. In Ayodhya

Sumanthra returned in the empty chariot with a heavy heart. He went straight to King Dasaratha's presence. Sumanthra was deeply grieved to see the King barely alive.

"Have you come back after leaving my Rama in the forest? O Rama! How can I live without you?" Dasaratha moaned and lapsed into unconsciousness.

Kausalya and Sumitra sat by the old King's bedside. Dasaratha recalled an episode in his past and recounted it to the grieving women.

Once, in his youth, he had gone hunting. He was skilled in shooting an arrow at game by mere sound. Dasaratha heard a gurgling noise and thought that it was a wild animal which had come to drink water at the river. He shot an arrow and ran in the direction of the noise.

The Dasaratha's utter horror, he found that his arrow had hit a young "rishi", who had been filling a pitcher with water, and not a wild animal as he had thought.

"Sir, please forgive me! Who are you?" Dasaratha cried.

"My name is Shravan Kumar. You have killed me. My old blind parents will be waiting for me to fetch water for them. Take this pitcher to that hut there and go. But before that, please pull out the arrow and end my pain!" the "rishi" gasped.

Dasaratha's hands trembled as he obeyed. With a sigh, the young "rishi" fell dead. Dasaratha picked up the pitcher and went in the direction Shravan Kumar had pointed out.

"O son Shravan! Why are you so late in bringing the water?" the old man called out when Dasaratha entered the hut.

"Please forgive me! I am King Dasaratha and not your son. I was out hunting and by mistake, I shot an arrow at your son who was by the riverside. He is dead. Please forgive me for the terrible sin, committed unknowingly!" Dasaratha's voice trembled with fear.

"What! Is our beloved son dead?" the old woman wailed.

Dasaratha felt helpless.

"Please take us to him at once!" the old man said.

Dasaratha carried the sightless old couple to the spot where Shravan Kumar lay. The old man asked Dasaratha to prepare a funeral pyre.

"What is the use of living when our sole support in old age has gone away? We do not wish to live anymore!" he cried.

"O King! As you have caused our son's death and have broken the hearts of his sightless old father and mother, you too will suffer similarly when you are separated from your son in old age, and die heartbroken with grief!" - the old woman cursed Dasaratha as husband and wife entered their son's funeral pyre.

Dasaratha now told Kausalya that he was paying for his past sin as he was separated from his beloved son in his old age and was losing his sense of sight too. He moaned the name of Rama frequently as he lay in his great bed. Towards midnight, when Kausalya and Sumitra had fallen into an exhausted slumber, King Dasaratha passed away quietly.

His death was discovered only the next morning when the ministers came to wake the King with the usual music.

16. Bharata's Home-coming

News about Dasaratha's death spread all over the city. The people of Ayodhya wept with fresh grief. They wondered what would happen.

The last rites of the departed King could not be performed as Rama and Lakshmana had gone to the forest, while Bharata and Shatrughna were away at Kekaya. So, the ministers decided to keep the body of the King immersed in oil till Bharata returned to Ayodhya.

Sage Vasishta sent for messengers and said, "Go swiftly to Kekaya to fetch Bharata here at once! Do not reveal in your manner or speech, all that has happened recently in Ayodhya - Rama's exile to the forest leading to the death of King Dasaratha!"

Bharata was puzzled to see the gloomy atmosphere in Ayodhya when he returned. The people he saw looked very dejected and mournful. Bharata went first to his father's palace on arrival and found it empty. So, he went to see his mother who was waiting for him eagerly. Bharata felt worried - he could not say why.

"Where is my father? I want to pay my respects to him!" he said.

"Son Bharata, your father led a fulfilled life with the usual joys and sorrows. Now he has gone to join his ancestors", Kaikeyi replied.

Bharata let out a loud cry of grief and fell down weeping like a child.

"Come on, son Bharata! It is not becoming of a King to cry like a child. Stand upright and perform all the duties which lie ahead of you!" Kaikeyi remarked.

Bharata did not hear his mother's words.

"O Mother! Did father suffer a lot? How lucky Rama is to have been beside father when he died! What were father's last words? Where is Rama, I must see him at once!" Bharata said.

Kaikeyi did not know what to reply. She thought for some time and said at last, "The last words your father said were 'O Rama! Will I see you when you come back?'"

"Why, where was Rama?" asked Bharata.

"Rama was not beside your father when he died, but far away in the forest with Sita and Lakshmana", said Kaikeyi.

Bharata wanted to know why Rama was in the forest. His mother was compelled to admit the part she had played in the matter - how she had asked King Dasaratha for two long-promised boons - one being that her own son, Bharata, should be crowned as the future King and the second boon being that Rama should go to the forest in exile for fourteen years.

"Stop worrying about Rama and concentrate on the tasks ahead! You must complete the funeral rites and then ascend the throne!" Kaikeyi urged.

"What have you done, mother? How can a younger son ascend the throne which rightfully belongs to the eldest son? O mother! Your actions have brought shame to the illustrious Ishvaku line - you have caused the death of your own husband! I am ashamed to call you my mother! I shall perform the last rites of the King, but as soon as possible, I shall go to the forest and bring Rama back to Ayodhya", Bharata stated firmly.

He hastened to Queen Kausalya's apartment to beg for pardon for the sin his mother had committed.

When Kausalya saw him, she said softly, "O Bharata! Do not have any fear about Sumitra and me - we shall not prevent you from ascending the throne. But we have one prayer - please let us join Rama in the forest! What is life here without him!"

Once again Bharata began weeping as he realised how much misery had been caused by his mother. He told her that he was totally innocent... that he loved Rama more than himself... that he would complete the funeral rites and then leave for the forest to bring Rama back to Ayodhya.

Bharata's sincere grief convinced Kausalya of his innocence.

17. Rama Journeys On

Rama, Sita and Lakshmana alighted from the boat after crossing the Ganga. Now, for the first time, they were totally alone, without being surrounded by anyone.

Rama told Lakshmana to go first. Sita would follow, and he, Rama, would walk behind her. Then she would be protected.

Sita was enchanted by everything she saw - the brightly-coloured flowers, the green leaves of the forest, the colourful birds and butterflies and the timid animals like the deer and the squirrels.

"O! please let us stay in this beautiful place!" she begged Rama.

Rama looked about and saw smoke coming from a human dwelling nearby.

"That will be an ashrama. Let us go and find out which place will be suitable for us to stay!" he said.

They all walked on and reached the ashrama. It belonged to Sage Bharadwaja. He welcomed them warmly.

"O revered Sage! Please can you tell us where we can live nearby in some safety?" Rama asked. "This place is very beautiful!"

Sage Bharadwaja agreed with Rama that the forest was beautiful and advised them to stay in the Chitrakoota region.

"Build a hut there. With my blessings you shall pass the years of your exile peacefully", he raised his hand in blessing as the three of them took leave to proceed to Chitrakoota.

Lakshmana skilfully built a thatched hut with the materials he found in the forest. Rama and Sita praised him for his effort.

So, here Rama, Sita and Lakshmana lived peacefully by the Chitrakoota hill.

18. Bharata Meets Rama

After all the funeral ceremonies were conducted in a fitting manner in memory of the famed King Dasaratha, Bharata called a meeting of Sage Vasishta and other ministers.

"O Bharata! You have to take up the reins of monarchy", said Sage Vasishta. "For, Ayodhya cannot remain without a ruler!"

Bharata respectfully declined and said that the throne rightfully belonged to Rama. How could a younger son succeed to the throne?

"I shall go to the forest and beg Rama to come back to Ayodhya. If he does not agree, I shall stay there performing penance for the wrongs done!" he declared.

Everyone applauded the noble-minded Bharata to whom Rama was life itself. By now, Kaikeyi had realised too late her folly and bitterly regretted the harm she had caused.

Preparations began immediately for Bharata's journey to the forest. Accompanied by Shatrughna, the three widowed Queens, the ministers and a large army, Bharata went to the forest.

As they reached the Tamasa river, Guha, the hunter chieftain became alarmed. He wondered if Bharata was following Rama with his army and had evil intent.

But conversation with Bharata revealed a different story. Guha was convinced that Bharata was intent on persuading Rama to return to Ayodhya. Guha was greatly relieved and offered all help at once.

"Rama has crossed the Ganga with Sita and Lakshmana", he informed Bharata.

Bharata immediately ordered his army to cross the river. They marched forward till they reached Sage Bharadwaja's ashrama.

Bharata went to the ashrama accompanied only by Sage Vasishta. He was overjoyed to learn from Sage Bharadwaja that Rama was living nearby in the Chitrakoota region.

"O Sage Bharadwaja, I am proceeding to meet Rama and beg him to return to Ayodhya. The throne belongs to him by right, and not to me! Please give me your blessings!" he said.

"O Bharata! I know how pure-hearted you are? I bless you in your task!" said the Sage. Bharata asked the widowed Queens to come forward to receive the Sage's blessings too.

Bharata described Queen Kausalya as the sorrowing mother of Rama, who was being supported by Queen Sumitra, the mother of Lakshmana and Shatrughna. Bharata described his own mother, Queen Kaikeyi, as the cause of all the sorrow.

Sage Bharadwaja looked with pity at the repentant Queen Kaikeyi and chided Bharata for speaking harshly about her.

"Go in that direction!" Sage Bharadwaja pointed.

Lakshmana, who was out gathering wild fruits, noticed that the birds in the place seemed to be disturbed by something and climbed up a tall tree to see what had happened. He saw Bharata walking at the head of a large army. Lakshmana at once ran to Rama and told him that Bharata was coming to kill him.

Rama listened to Lakshmana and smiled. "You are wrong about Bharata, Lakshmana! I know Bharata and his gentle upright nature, the immense love he has for me. I am sure Bharata is coming here to beg me to return to Ayodhya. So, do not talk ill of him!"

As Rama had predicted, Bharata, dressed in the garb of an ascetic, walked barefoot and fell at Rama's feet with tears in his eyes.

"How is our beloved father? Why have you left him to come here?" Rama asked affectionately.

"O brother Rama! Our father is no more!" Bharata cried.

On hearing this, Rama fell unconscious. When he recovered, he said, "O Bharata! how unfortunate I am to be denied the right to perform his funeral rites!"

Accompanied by Sage Vasishta, Rama, Lakshmana, Bharata and Shatrughna, as well as the three widowed Queens, went to nearby river to offer water to the departed King.

Back at the hut, Bharata fell at Rama's feet and begged him to return to Ayodhya and accept the kingship. He said that he himself would serve the 14-year exile sentence.

"No, Bharata. If I do so, I will be breaking our father's promise. Do you think that our father's soul will be happy? No, I cannot return to Ayodhya!" Rama replied gently but firmly.

Then Bharata requested Rama to give him his "padukas" which would be installed on the throne.

"I will go to Nandigramam and lead the life of an ascetic and do penance till you return. I shall rule from there on your behalf. But if you do not return, I shall jump into the fire!" Bharata declared.

"Do not worry, Bharata! The fourteen years will speed by and I shall return to Ayodhya", Rama said.

Then Bharata placed Rama's "padukas" on his head and departed. The people of Ayodhya realised now how much Bharata loved Rama and did not mind being under his rule.

19. Rama To The Rescue

After Bharata's departure, Rama felt extremely sad. He saw the image of Bharata's dejected face everywhere he looked. So, he decided to go further on and help the sages who were being troubled by the rakshasas.

Rama, Sita and Lakshmana entered the Dandaka forest. Suddenly a hideous distorted figure of a rakshasa stood in their path.

"I am the great Viraada. Who are you, you little men dressed like ascetics but accompanied by a woman?" he roared angrily and caught hold of Sita.

"Surely Kaikeyi must have been aware that life in the forest would be full of unexpected dangers!" Lakshmana burst out angrily.

Rama and Lakshmana shot countless arrows at him. But Viraada had obtained a boon from Lord Brahma that no weapon could kill him. So, Rama's and Lakshmana's arrows just bounced off Viraada.

But one arrow pierced Viraada. He howled with pain and put down Sita. Viraada then lifted Rama and Lakshmana and put them on his shoulders. He walked off into the forest, without another glance at Sita who wept.

Rama and Lakshmana then broke off his arms. The rakshasa threw them on the ground and writhed with pain. Rama then put his foot on Viraada. At the touch of Rama's foot, Viraada could feel the curse he was under lifting.

"O Lord! At the touch of your holy foot, I can recall my past. I am really a Gandharva and was cursed to

become a rakshasa. Please kill me without weapons so that I will be free!" Viraada begged.

So, Rama and Lakshmana broke all his bones and buried him in a pit which they dug.

They then went back to the place where Sita was and told her everything. After this episode, Rama and Lakshmana took it on themselves to rid the Dandaka forest of the rakshasas who tormented the sages who lived there. A decade passed by in this manner.

20. Enter Surpanakha

Rama, Sita and Lakshmana decided to move on. On the advice of Sage Agasthya, whose ashrama they visited, the three of them went to a forest, Panchavati, on the bank of the Godavari river. Sita greatly appreciated the natural beauty she saw everywhere she looked. So, Rama asked Lakshmana to construct a hut for them to live in.

One day, Rama and Lakshmana were out hunting and saw a huge figure on a tree, which they thought belonged to a rakshasa. On closer look, however, Rama and Lakshmana found that it was a huge eagle.

"Who are you?" Rama asked.

"I am Jataayu, the son of the God of Dawn, Aruna. My brother is Sampaati. O Rama! I am your father's old friend. Whenever you leave Sita alone, I shall look after her carefully!" he said.

Some time after this, a rakshasi, named Surpanakha, came to Panchavati. She hid behind a tree to see who was living in the hut. When she saw Rama, she fell in love with him at once.

Unaware of the hideous picture she presented, Surpanakha walked up to Rama and asked him who he was. On learning that he was Rama, the son of King Dasaratha of Ayodhya, the rakshasi boasted, "I am Surpanakha, the only sister of the mighty King of Lanka, Ravana.

Kumbakarna, Vibheeshana are my brothers, while Khara and Dooshana, who live in the Janasthana area, are also my brothers. O Rama! I have fallen in love with you. Marry me at once. Do not consider my ugly form. I can change my shape to look beautiful for you!"

Rama laughed gently and said, "O Surpanakha! I am already married to that lady there. How can I marry you? See my brother, Lakshmana? He is handsome and strong. Ask him to marry you - he is not accompanied by a woman like me. Besides, you are a princess and I am a mere ascetic!"

So, Surpanakha went to Lakshmana and asked him to marry her. Lakshmana laughed loudly and said, "O Surpanakha! Rama is joking! He is really a prince and I am his servant. How can you, a princess, marry a servant? Go back and ask him again!"

Surpanakha returned to Rama and asked him once again to marry her. But once again he said that he has already married. Surpanakha grew angry and shouted that she would kill Sita as she stood in her way.

Lakshmana immediately took out his sword and cut her nose off. Surpanakha screamed with pain as blood streamed down her face and ran to Janasthana.

21. Rama Slays The Rakshasa Hordes

"O brothers, Khara and Dooshana! Look at what Rama and Lakshmana have done to me!" she wailed then she saw her brothers. "Go and avenge my pain!"

Khara sent his rakshasa warriors and went to Panchavati with Surpanakha. But Rama and Lakshmana killed them all easily. Greatly angered, Khara and Dooshana themselves led a great army of thousands of strong rakshasas.

"Do not worry, Surpanakha! We have never been defeated in battle and will win now too. We will kill Rama and Lakshmana to avenge the humiliation you have suffered at their hands!" Khara boasted as they set out.

Rama and Lakshmana saw the rakshasa hordes approaching. Then Rama told his brother to take Sita to a safe place while he fought with rakshasas. He assured Lakshmana that he could tackle the rakshasas single-handedly.

That was exactly what Rama did. Within a short time he destroyed the entire rakshasa army single-handed. Then, with sharp arrows he killed Khara and Dooshana too. The Devas and rishis who were watching the battle, blessed Rama by showering petals from above. They rejoiced that Rama had rid the Dandaka forest of rakshasas and so brought peace to the region.

In the meanwhile, Surpanakha, who had witnessed the slaying of her brothers, Khara and Dooshana and their mighty rakshasa army, fled to Lanka. She created a sensation when she ran into the court over which the resplendent ten-headed Ravana, her brother, presided. Everyone was totally shocked to see the blood streaming from Surpanakha's mutilated nose.

"O brother Ravana, here you are sitting supremely unaware that your brothers Khara and Dooshana and all the rakshasas in Janasthana have been killed by mere humans, Rama and Lakshmana. All because I tried to get Rama's wife, Sita, for you!"

"O brother Ravana! The moment I saw Sita, I knew that she was a jewel fit to adorn your court. I cannot describe Sita's beauty!" Surpanakha lied, wanting to take revenge on Rama and Lakshmana. "It would be good if you managed to get hold of Sita. For if Rama is separated from her, he is sure to die!"

Ravana remembered how he had tried to string the bow of Siva and so win Sita's hand in marriage. He had been unable to even lift and left the hall which resounded with laughter. But he had not forgotten Sita's beauty.

"Do not worry, Surpanakha! I will teach Rama and Lakshmana a fitting lesson by kidnapping Sita!" Ravana told his sister. He flew in his chariot to the place where his kinsman, Mareecha, lived. Mareecha, who was Taataka's son, now lived like a hermit.

"O Mareecha! I want to take revenge on Rama and Lakshmana who cut off my sister, Surpanakha's nose, by kidnapping Rama's wife, Sita!" he said.

Mareecha, who remembered the might of Rama and Lakshmana, trembled at the very name, Rama.

"O King Ravana! Who gave you this bad advice? Sita belongs to another man. You should not carry her away by force. It means inviting your own death. Go back to Lanka and forget the matter", Mareecha said. "Rama and Lakshmana were mere boys when they defeated Subanu and me. Now they are grown men and mighty warriors!"

But Ravana would not listen.

"O Mareecha! I am not asking you to face Rama's arrows. You have magic powers and can take any shape. All I want you to take the form of a beautiful golden deer and prance about playfully so that Sita can see you. She will definitely want you and will ask Rama and Lakshmana to catch you. I want you to move away from hut and so take Rama and Lakshmana deeper into the forest. Then I shall take away Sita!" Ravana revealed his plan to Mareecha.

Mareecha's face turned pale as he tried once again to change Ravana's mind. But he failed. With a deep sigh, he decided that it would be better if he died at Rama's hand rather than at Ravana's. So, he agreed.

22. The Golden Deer

Ravana and Mareecha flew in Ravana's golden chariot to Panchavati. Ravana hid behind some trees and ordered Mareecha to play his part.

Sita was busy plucking flowers for their daily worship when she saw a beautiful golden deer nibbling at the grass near their hut. She at once called Rama and Lakshmana to see the beautiful creature. They saw the golden deer and admired it, and agreed with Sita that it was really a beautiful animal.

"Please can you catch it for me, my Lord! I want to take it back to Ayodhya and keep it as a pet!" Sita begged.

Rama, like all husbands, wanted to please his lovely wife. So, he agreed at once to chase it. But Lakshmana was more cautious.

"Brother, I do not think that it is really a deer, but a rakshasa in disguise!" he warned.

This only made Sita more determined to get the golden deer. So, she begged Rama once more to get it for her.

Rama felt that even if Lakshmana was right and that the deer was really a rakshasa, he would be able to kill the rakshasa easily. And, if it was a

deer which could not be caught, he could kill it and give the skin to Sita. So, he agreed to go after the golden deer.

"Lakshmana, you must stand on guard here. Do not, on any account, leave Sita alone!" Rama said before he went.

This was the very chance Mareecha had been waiting for. As the golden deer, he sprang nimbly away each time Rama came near. Gradually the two of them went further and further into the forest.

Then, Mareecha, tiring of the chase, stood still so that Rama's arrow pierced him. As he fell, he assumed his original rakshasa form and cried loudly in a voice which sounded like Rama's "O Lakshmana! O Sita!"

At once Rama realised that Lakshmana's guess was correct. The golden deer was really a rakshasa. But Rama felt confident that Lakshmana would not leave Sita alone even for a moment. But he ran back to the hut.

Little did he know what was happening at the hut. Sita and Lakshmana had heard (What they thought was Rama's voice) crying "O Lakshmana! O Sita!"

"O Lakshmana! That was Rama crying for help. Do go quickly and find out what is wrong!" Sita begged.

"Do not worry! Rama can cope with any rakshasa single-handed. He will not need any help and will be terribly angry with me if I leave you alone, unprotected" Lakshmana replied.

"Lakshmana! Once again, I order you to go to Rama's help!" Sita repeated.

Lakshmana stood still as if he had not heard Sita's command.

Sita began sobbing wildly. "Now I know that you are Rama's enemy. You pretended to accompany us to the forest in order to get rid of Rama and then disgrace me. If you do not go, I shall end my life" she cried.

Lakshmana was deeply hurt by Sita's unjust accusations.

"All right, I will go! But before that I shall draw a line outside the hut which you must not cross for your own safety!" Lakshmana said reluctantly and with the tip of his arrow, he drew a wide circle around the hut.

Then he went away looking back uneasily.

23. Ravana Abducts Sita

The stage was now set for Ravana to enter the scene. He waited till Lakshmana disappeared from sight. Ravana then assumed the form of a sannyasi who chanted holy vedic verses and called loudly for alms.

Sita, who was hovering near the doorway of the hut waiting for Lakshmana to return with Rama, saw the sannyasi and heard his request for alms. She went in to fetch a bowl of rice which she held out. But the sannyasi, who was really Ravana in disguise, knew that it would be dangerous to cross the line drawn by Lakshmana. So, he said, "Come, my daughter, come near and receive my blessings!"

"O revered Sir! Please accept my offering. I cannot cross this line and come out" Sita explained.

"Then I shall go elsewhere to seek alms!" the sannyasi remarked and turned as if to go away.

Sita felt ashamed of herself for trying to ignore a holy man's request for alms and slowly stepped over the line which Lakshmana had drawn. At once the sannyasi revealed his true form. He grabbed Sita's hand and pulled her forward.

"Come with me, my beautiful one and be Ravana's Queen! Why should you waste your beauty and time with poor Rama who has been exiled to the forest? Come with me to Lanka and live the life of luxury!" he said.

Sita struggled in his grasp and said, "Alas! Why did I send Lakshmana away! Let me go at once. Rama and Lakshmana will come and soon slay you!"

Ravana just laughed and pushed Sita into his golden chariot.

As they flew upward, Sita cried as loudly as she could, "O Rama! O Lakshmana! Please help me! Save me from this wicked rakshasa who is carrying me away to Lanka! Help, O Rama! O Lakshmana!"

24. Brave Jataayu

Sita's cries woke Jataayu who was perched on a tree nearby. He flapped his huge wings and flew over Ravana's chariot.

"O Ravana! I am Jataayu, the son of God of Dawn, Aruna! You must first fight with me for I shall not let you kidnap another man's wife, the beautiful Sita."

Then began a great battle between Ravana and the brave Jataayu, the King of eagles. He clawed Ravana with sharp talons. Deeply wounded and bleeding from his wounds, Ravana slashed at Jataayu with his sword and inflicted deep cuts on him. Jataayu tried to wrench off Ravana's arms which held Sita. But the rakshasa had twenty arms - when one was cut off another grew in its place to the eagle's dismay.

Jataayu was of and unarmed and tiring of the unequal fight. But he gathered strength somehow and killed Ravana's steeds and his charioteer. In revenge, Ravana chopped off Jataayu's powerful wings. The brave old bird fell on the ground and could not move.

Sita shed tears of despair and sorrow. She thanked the old bird for trying to help her despite the danger to his own life.

"O Rama! O Lakshmana! Please come soon and save me!" she cried helplessly. Sita tried to run away.

But Ravana caught hold of her and rose in the air. As they flew over the Pampa river, Sita saw some monkey like beings standing on a hill top. She took off her jewels, wrapped them in her sash and threw the bundle down. Sita hoped that Rama would somehow see and recognize them...that they would give him a clue about the direction in which she was being carried away.

Ravana crossed the vast see with Sita and entered the island-city of Lanka.

"Agree to my demand and you will not suffer!" Ravana said.

Sita laughed and replied, "Ravana, I was married to Rama in the presence of the holy fire and will accept only him and no other man. Do not desire me. Rama will come soon with Lakshmana and destroy you!"

Ravana was greatly enraged.

"Who is there!" he called for his rakshasi guards. "Take Sita to the Asoka Vana! Give her whatever she wants, make her change her mind, but do not let her escape!" he turned to Sita and ordered her to go with the rakshasis.

The Asoka Vana was a very beautiful park with plenty of trees and flowering shrubs and fountains. Birds and butterflies flew about gaily. Sita did not see them as she sat under an asoka tree. She was totally sunk in grief.

25. Rama's Grief

After killing Mareecha, Rama hastened back to the hut. On the way he met Lakshmana running towards him and he said quite angrily, "O Lakshmana! Why have you left Sita alone and come here instead? As you rightly guessed, the golden deer was really a rakshasa. I fear that something has happened to Sita! Oh, why did you leave her, Lakshmana? Let us go back quickly to the hut!"

As they ran, Lakshmana told his brother how Sita had accused him of all intention and had forced him to go to her husband's help as she had threatened to end her life otherwise. When Rama and Lakshmana reached the hut, they found it empty and saw the scattered rice, flowers and the upturned kamandalam. They knew at once that Sita had been kidnapped by someone.

Rama wept inconsolably and Lakshmana tried to comfort him.

"Let us search for her. Perhaps she has gone to collect flowers!" Lakshmana suggested.

Rama and Lakshmana called loudly for Sita as they searched everywhere. Suddenly they came upon a huge figure lying on the ground. It was the wounded Jataayu, the King of the eagles.

"O Rama! I saw Ravana off with Sita in his chariot and attacked him when she begged me to help. We fought for long, but I was tiring as I am getting old. Ravana then chopped off my wings and I fell on the ground. I have been lying here, waiting to tell you about Ravana!" Jataayu gasped, gland that he could help Rama in a small way. The brave old bird died soon after.

Rama and Lakshmana wept and they performed the funeral rites for Jataayu as they would have done for their own father.

26. Kabandha's Advice

Then the two brothers moved on and searched for anyone who could tell them where Ravana had gone with Sita. Suddenly a grotesque-looking figure of a rakshasa with only one eye in the middle of his chest, his mouth in huge stomach, and two enormous arms, confronted them. The creature just stretched out his arms and caught Rama and Lakshmana, without moving even an inch from his position.

"I shall cut off one arm and you do likewise with the other arm" Rama told Lakshmana.

The creature became helpless without his arms and asked who his attackers were.

"We are princes of Ayodhya. My name is Rama and this is my brother, Lakshmana. My wife, Sita has been kidnapped by Ravana. We are searching for her" Rama said. "Who are you and what is your name?"

"My name is Kabandha. I was really a Gandharva and was cursed by Indra to become a monster. Indra told me that I would be free of the curse only if I met you both. He said that you would cut off my arms and consign my body to the flames. So, please will you light a fire?" Kabandha asked.

Rama and Lakshmana set fire to his body and from the flames rose a celestial being.

"O Rama! Listen closely to what I say. With the help of my powers, I can see that you will regain Sita. Go further south. In the Rishyamooka Hill on the bank of the Pampa river, the fugitive vaanara prince Sugriva lives there in exile as he was driven out of the kingdom by his brother Vali. Gain Sugriva's friendship and you will surely succeed!" Saying this, the celestial being rose in the air and vanished. Rama and Lakshmana felt comforted. Now they knew in which direction they should go. As they neared the Pampa river, they came to the ashram of Sabari.

Sabari was a saintly woman and a great disciple of sage Matanga. When he was about to die, she wished to depart from the world too. But sage Matanga advised her to wait for the arrival of Vishnu in his Rama avataar and obtain his blessings.

So, Sabari gathered wild fruits and kept them in the ashram in anticipation of Rama's arrival. When Rama came, she lovingly gave him the fruits she had gathered. With his permission, she kindled a fire and entered it and attained the heavens.

27. Rama Meets Hanuman

Rama felt greatly encouraged after this meeting and was sure that he would succeed in his search for Sita. He went with Lakshmana all over the forest on Rishyamooka hill in search of Sugriva.

The exiled vaanara prince, Sugriva and his followers saw Rama and Lakshmana. They became worried in case the two men were really Vali's followers and had come to kill them. Sugriva asked his trusted minister, Hanuman to go in the guise of a scholar and find out who they were.

The moment Hanuman met Rama, he experienced a thrill of complete delight and bliss. All pretence fell away and he introduced himself as Hanuman, the son of Vayu, the God of Winds, and the trusted minister of Sugriva, the vaanara Prince.

"O Hanuman! We are very glad to meet the confidante of the person whom we are seeking, Sugriva. I am Rama, and this is my brother, Lakshmana. We are the sons of King Dasaratha of Ayodhya. Because of a promise made to his youngest Queen, Kaikeyi, and in order to keep my father's word, I was exiled to the forest for fourteen years, and was accompanied by my brother, Lakshmana, and my wife Sita. We lived happily in Panchavati till my wife Sita was kidnapped by Ravana of Lanka. We need Sugriva's help to get Sita back!" said Rama. Lakshmana asked Hanuman why Sugriva was living in exile.

28. Sugriva's Sad Story

Hanuman then told the princes of Ayodhya that Vali, the vaanara King of Kishkinda had a young brother called Sugriva. Vali was a mighty warrior. Once a rakshasa named Maaya, challenged Vali to fight. The fight went on for days. Maaya suddenly disappeared into a cave. Vali and Sugriva chased him. Vali bade Sugriva to stand on guard at the mouth of the cave and went in.

Sugriva stood outside for a long time and heard the sounds of battle going on in the cave. Vali did not emerge, but a stream of blood began to flow out of the cave. Sugriva at once thought Vali had been killed. He was afraid that Maaya would come out. So, he rolled a huge boulder and blocked the cave's entrance.

Then he returned to Kishkinda. The ministers urged him to assume kingship. Sugriva agreed. Months later, a tired looking Vali reached Kishkinda. He angrily accused Sugriva of deliberately blocking the mouth of the cave. Vali would not listen when Sugriva repeatedly said that he was innocent...that he had thought Maaya had killed Vali, so he had blocked the entrance of the cave out of sheer fear.

"You are lying!" Vali shouted and drove Sugriva out of Kishkinda depriving him of his wife, home and all his possessions.

Now Sugriva was living in safety at Rishyamooka hill with his followers as he had learned that Vali could not come there because of a curse. Once, Vali has insulted the sage Matanga whose ashram was in the Rishyamooka area. The sage cursed him with death, if he, Vali, ever set foot in the Rishyamooka area.

"That is why prince Sugriva feels safe here. He has asked me to bring you to him!" Hanuman said. As the way to Sugriva's cave quite a difficult one, Hanuman carried Rama and Lakshmana on his shoulders.

29. Rama Vows To Help Sugriva

"O Prince Sugriva, Hanuman has told us your sad story. I hereby vow that I will fight with Vali so that you regain Kishkinda!" Rama declared.

"And I vow that I will help you to search for your kidnapped wife, Sita. I have just remembered! Hanuman, do you recall the time when we saw a rakshasa flying in the air with a crying woman? She threw a bundle of her jewels, which we have kept safely. O Prince Rama! Please can you see and identify them?" Sugriva exclaimed.

Rama wept when Sugriva handed the bundle to him.

"O Lakshmana! I cannot bear to look at the jewels!" he cried.

Lakshmana took a look at the jewels in the bundle.

"I am certain that these are her anklets because I bowed at her feet every morning! I am not so sure about the other jewels" he said at once.

Rama's grief turned into burning rage.

"I will not rest till I kill Ravana" he vowed.

On seeing Rama's intense emotion, Sugriva and the other vaanaras became worried in case Rama forgot his promise to help Sugriva regain Kishkinda. So Sugriva decided to remind Rama in a roundabout way.

"O Lord Rama! It is very sad for you to be reminded how cruelly you have been separated from your beloved wife! I will definitely find out the exact strength of Ravana and will help you to recover Sita. Do not grieve! Think how I have managed to keep my courage up despite being exiled like you!" Sugriva said with feeling.

Rama felt encouraged on hearing these words.

30. Sugriva's Sudden Doubt

Sugriva and all the vaanaras were greatly relieved that Rama had decided to help them first by fighting with Vali. Sugriva looked at Rama's graceful figure with doubt.

"O Lord Rama! Though I do not doubt your ability with weapons, I must tell you that my brother, Vali, is a very strong, mighty warrior. Let me tell you about his great strength…"

"Once a great buffalo-asura, named Dundubi, who had the strength of a thousand elephants, challenged anyone who dared, for a fight. He found no worthy opponent but Vali. Dundubi went to Kishkinda and stood before Vali's palace."

"O Vali! Much have I heard about your strength. Come out and fight with me if you dare!" Dundubi bellowed tauntingly.

"Vali came rushing out of the palace. He caught hold of the buffalo-asura's tail and whirled him in the air. Then he flung Dundubi on the ground. But the asura recovered and fought with Vali. In the end, Vali pounded Dundubi to death and flung the death carcass of the buffalo-asura to a far-away place."

"Many drops of blood from Dundubi's carcass were carried by the wind and these fell on sage Matanga's ashram in Rishyamooka, polluting it. Sage Matanga was furious with Vali and cursed him saying that he would die at once if he ever dared to set foot in the Rishyamooka region."

"That is why I am safe in this Rishyamooka area. Vali cannot come here" Sugriva said.

Rama smiled gently and with a kick of his toe, he sent the huge skeleton of Dundubi which was lying nearby, flying into the air to a great distance.

However, Sugriva was not satisfied and stated that when Vali had flung the carcass, it was heavy as it was full of flesh and blood, not a weather-beaten old skeleton.

Then Rama took up his mighty bow and walked to nearby line of trees. With a single arrow, he pierced seven of them. The arrow emerged only to pierce the ground on the other side deeply. Now Sugriva was fully convinced of Rama's strength.

31. Rama Slays Vali

So, Sugriva went boldly to Kishkinda and stood before Vali's palace. "Ho Vali! Come out and fight with me!" he shouted.

With an angry roar, Vali emerged. He and Sugriva wrestled for a long time as both brothers were very strong and brave. Sugriva waited for Rama to strike.

But, Rama, who was hiding behind a tree, was utterly puzzled. Both Sugriva and Vali looked very much alike in form and face. So, he could not say which was Vali and which was Sugriva. So, he did not shoot an arrow.

In the meantime, Sugriva got the worst of the fight and ran away bleeding profusely from his wounds to the safety of the Rishyamooka forest. He was furious when he saw Rama.

"O Rama! I did not expect such behaviour from you! If you did not wish to kill Vali, why did you not say so? Then I would not have challenged him at all! I trusted you and all I got was a severe beating!" he said bitterly.

"O Sugriva! Do not be so angry, but listen to my problem. I could not shoot an arrow in case I killed the wrong one – you and Vali are so much alike that I was very puzzled and helpless. Go

again and challenge Vali to a fight. But this time, wear this garland of creepers around your neck so that I will know which is Vali", explained Rama patiently.

So, Sugriva wore the garland of creepers and went to challenge Vali.

Vali was in the company of his wise wife, Tara, when Sugriva's voice reached them.

"I suspect something, my Lord! Why should Sugriva come here again to challenge you, knowing fully well that you can defeat him easily? Sugriva must be having a secret weapon!" she warned.

Vali brushed aside her words and went out. Sugriva was filled with fresh confidence and fought bravely with Vali. However he soon began to tire. This was the moment Rama was waiting for, as he hid behind a tree. He shot a deadly arrow which pierced Vali's chest.

Vali fell bleeding, fatally wounded. He saw Rama approaching with his bow in his hand and reproached him. "O Rama! How could you act so meanly against dharma and shoot an arrow at one engaged in combat with another? Did you know that this necklace which I am wearing was given to me by Indra, protects me from opponents who face me in combat, and so hid behind a tree? I did not expect such a base attitude from a member of the illustrious Ishvaku line. If you wanted help against Ravana, I would have willingly fought and defeated him easily!"

Rama laughed gently and replied, "O Vali! It is not proper for you to talk about dharma. Were you righteous when you would not even give Sugriva a chance to explain his part of the story, but drove your own brother from Kishkinda and deprived

him of his wife too? Sugriva is my dear friend and understand what it is to lose a wife!"

Vali could not reply to Rama's words. He looked around saw his weeping wife, and their son, Angada.

"O Angada! Sugriva will take care of you now. Look at him and obey him as you would do to your own father. Tara, do not grieve! Sugriva, do not grieve! Take this necklace which our father, Indra, gave me. It will protect you from enemies!" saying this, Vali breathed his last.

Angada performed his father's last rites, helped by a remorseful Sugriva who repented being the cause of his own brother's death.

32. Sugriva Is Reminded Of His Promise

Rama and Lakshmana continued to live in a cave in the Rishyamooka hill after Sugriva was crowned King of Kishkinda and Angada was crowned Yuvaraja. Sugriva's new-found power and freedom made him indulge in all kinds of merry making and he soon forgot about his promise to Rama. Hanuman, his wise minister, knew that Sugriva's attitude was wrong and gently tried to remind his King.

"Leave me alone, Hanuman! Rama and Lakshmana must be aware that nothing can be done in the rainy season we are experiencing. Just order all the vaanaras to assemble here soon!" Sugriva replied.

At last the rains stopped. But there was no sign of Sugriva coming to meet Rama.

Rama became angry and shouted at Lakshmana, "O Lakshmana! Go at once to the gates of Kishkinda and remind the ungrateful Sugriva about his promise made to me and warn him that the fate which overtook Vali can befall him too!"

Lakshmana too was furious with Sugriva. He strode to Sugriva's palace and twanged the string of his mighty bow loudly. The sound alerted Hanuman. It frightened Sugriva who sent Hanuman to calm the angry prince. Tara, Vali's widow, too went with him.

Lakshmana's anger abated somewhat when he saw them.

"O Lakshmana! Thank you for coming! I am sure that you will excuse Sugriva for celebrating his new position after being in exile for years!" said Tara.

"O Prince! King Sugriva has already ordered all the vaanaras to come here. Then he will meet Lord Rama to discuss the strategy in searching for Sita!" Hanuman added.

Lakshmana looked more calm. But he said, "O Hanuman, please tell your King that Rama is growing impatient!"

He then returned to the cave and told Rama what Tara and Hanuman had told him.

33. The Search For Sita Begins

All the vaanaras assembled at Kishkinda following Sugriva's orders. They all accompanied the vaanara King to the cave in the Rishyamooka hill. Sugriva bowed to Rama and asked him to speak to the crowd.

"O Sugriva! Our first goal should be to find out in which direction Sita was taken and where she is now. But you are the King of the vaanaras. So, you should issue the orders!" Rama embraced Sugriva as he said this.

Sugriva then ordered his generals to lead search parties in the four different directions and search everywhere to find the whereabouts of Sita.

Then he turned to his trusted advisor and minister, Hanuman and said, "O Son of Vaayu! I somehow feel that you will be the one to succeed in our task. Lead the search party southward and come back with good news!"

Rama too felt that Hanuman would be the one to find Sita. From the first meeting, Rama had been drawn to the son of Vaayu.

"O Hanuman! Here is my signet ring. Please give this to Sita when you find her. Tell her that I will come quickly and rescue her!" he said and handed over his signet ring to Hanuman.

Hanuman received the ring reverently and pressed it to his eyes. He bowed to Rama, Lakshmana and Sugriva before he set off to be the head of the vaanaras.

The vaanara parties which had travelled east, west and north returned within a month stipulated by Sugriva. None of them could find out where Sita was. But Rama, Lakshmana and Sugriva waited hopefully for Hanuman's search party which had gone south and had not returned.

34. Hanuman Travels Southward

The vaanara army led by Hanuman, Angada and Jambavan searched all over the hills and forests in the south. But they found no sign of Sita. They sat tired and hungry after an unsuccessful search. Suddenly they saw colourful birds flying out of a dark cave from which fragrant scents also came. They decided to enter the cave and search for food.

The vaanaras linked their hands and groped in the cave's darkness. They must have walked several miles till they saw a gleam of light which signified that they had reached the mouth of the cave. On emerging from the darkness, they came to a beautiful city, with streets paved with gold. The vaanaras saw an elderly sannyasini and bowed respectfully to her.

She first gave them refreshments to appease their hunger and thirst. When the vaanaras had eaten and drunk to their heart's content, she asked them who they were. The vaanaras bowed to her and said, "O holy one! We are all the subjects of Sugriva, King of Kishkinda. Sita, the wife of prince Rama of Ayodhya, was kidnapped by Ravana. We are searching for Sita. Our king has given us a month's time, but we have not succeeded so far and have lost a lot of time. Please tell us who you are!"

She told them that her name was Swayamprabha and that the city

she lived in had been built by Maaya, the architect of the Daanvas, who were the enemies of the Devas.

"Indra killed Maaya and gave the city to my friend, Hema. I am looking after it for her", Swayamprabha replied.

Then Swayamprabha told them that no one who entered the cave could leave it. But as they were engaged in an important task, she transported them to the seashore by her supernatural powers.

The vaanaras discovered that the time limit set by Sugriva had lapsed and were most dejected. Angada said mournfully that he was sure Sugriva would put them all to death if they went back without any information.

"It is better to die here by myself, I shall fast unto death here!" he declared and sat down on the ground.

The other vaanaras too wept as they joined Angada in his fast-unto-death resolve.

35. Sampaati's Tale

As the vaanaras were exchanging their stories of woe, regarding their failure to find Rama's wife, Sita... how she had been kidnapped by Ravana... how the brave Jataayu had tried to save her... a huge eagle with broken wings crawled out of a mountain-cave nearby. He was happy that he would be able to feed on so many vaanaras for days when they died without having to move.

Just then he heard Angada saying, "How fortunate Jataayu was! He could help Rama in a small way, though he was slain by Ravana! Brave Jataayu fought with Ravana to prevent him from taking Sita away. But Ravana cut off his wings and wounded him fatally!"

The old eagle was shocked. "O vaanaras! What is it that you are saying...is Jataayu really dead?" he cried.

Angada and the others went near and asked the eagle who he was.

"I am Sampaati, the elder brother of Jataayu. We are both sons of the God of Dawn, Aruna. I have not seen Jataayu for a long time. Once, when we were young, we both competed with each other to find out who could fly higher. As we neared the Sun, it scorched us and Jataayu was nearly burnt. So, I quickly spread my own wings protectively.

Though Jataayu was saved, my wings were burned and I fell on this hill. I have been living here, unable to move. I can help you, for I saw Ravana carrying Sita away!" he said.

"O Sampaati! Please can you tell us in which direction Ravana went so that we can help Rama?" asked Hanuman.

Sampaati's keen vision helped to see for miles around.

"Sita is in the park in Ravana's island-city Lanka!" he informed them. "It is across the sea."

At once new feathers sprouted from his body. He had been rewarded for helping Lord Rama! Sampaati was extremely delighted and flew away.

36. Hanuman Cross The Ocean

The vaanaras were wild with happiness now that they knew for certain where Sita was. But they were determined to see this with their own eyes. However a fresh problem arose – how could they cross the vast ocean to reach Lanka?

"I want each vaanara to stem forward to tell us how far he can jump! I myself can cross the ocean. But I will not have the strength to jump back!" said Angada.

One by one the vaanara announced different distances they could cover. Then, Jambavan, the aged vaanara leader, asked Hanuman why he was sitting apart silently.

"O Maaruti, son of the great Vaayu and Anjana, with your supreme strength, courage and wisdom, there is nothing which you cannot accomplish easily! You are a 'chiranjeevi' and death can come to you only when you will it. So, Hanuman, please get up and help not only us, but Rama! Arise, O son of Vaayu, and reveal your might to us all!"

At the reminder of his powers, Hanuman grew to gigantic proportions. Due to a curse by a rishi, when he was young, Hanuman could remember the full extent of his strength only when he was reminded of it by others.

Angada, Jambavan and the other vaanaras watched with awe as Hanuman grew till he reached the sky! Hanuman swished his tail and let out a mighty roar which resounded all over the three worlds as he climbed the Mahendra hill which would bear the weight of his foot as he prepared to jump.

Hanuman first bowed to all Devas to bless him when he began the important mission. Then he pressed down on the hill and rose in the sky, flying higher and higher with the passing of every second. He moved across the sky with the speed of the wind.

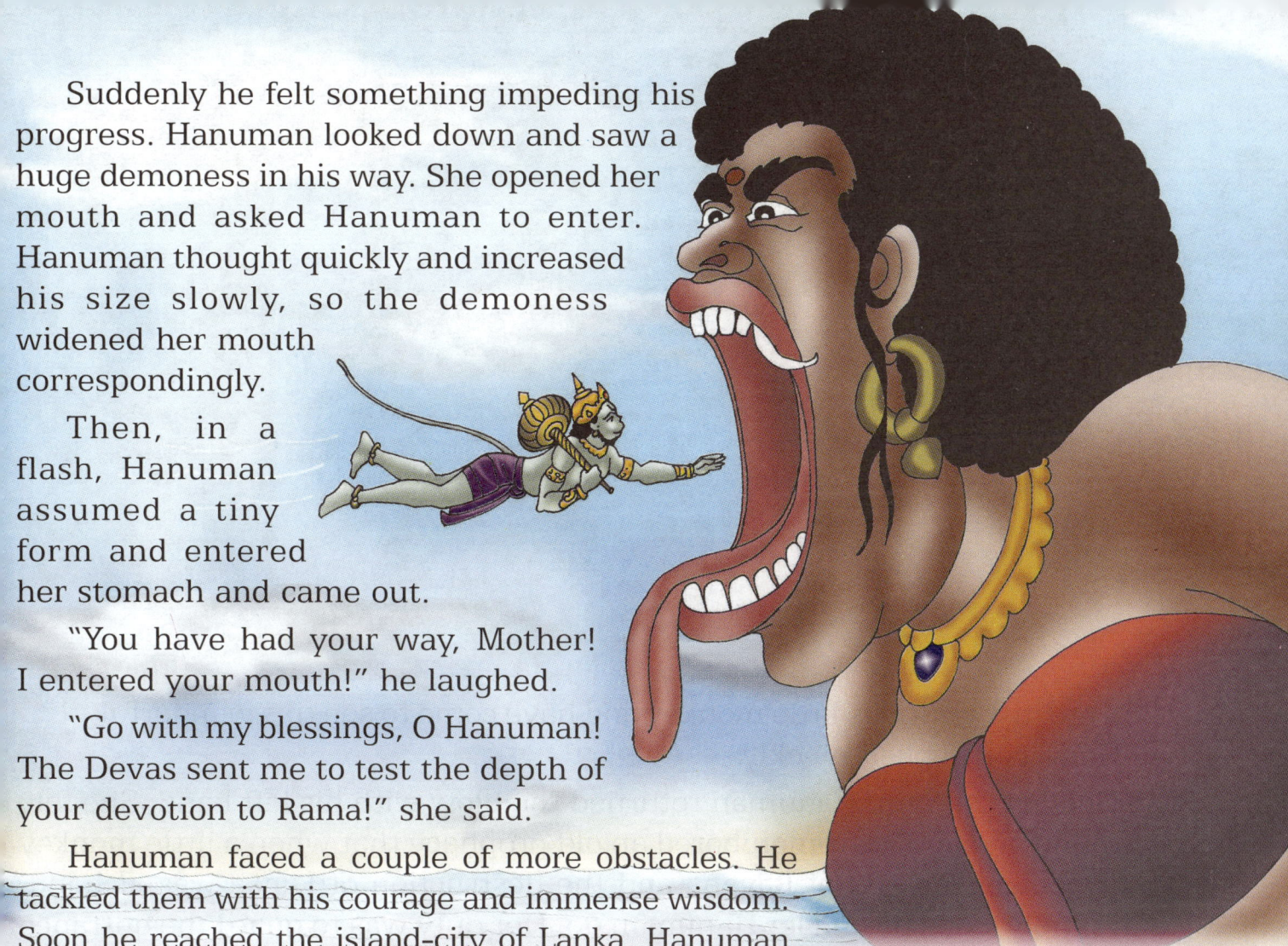

Suddenly he felt something impeding his progress. Hanuman looked down and saw a huge demoness in his way. She opened her mouth and asked Hanuman to enter. Hanuman thought quickly and increased his size slowly, so the demoness widened her mouth correspondingly.

Then, in a flash, Hanuman assumed a tiny form and entered her stomach and came out.

"You have had your way, Mother! I entered your mouth!" he laughed.

"Go with my blessings, O Hanuman! The Devas sent me to test the depth of your devotion to Rama!" she said.

Hanuman faced a couple of more obstacles. He tackled them with his courage and immense wisdom. Soon he reached the island-city of Lanka. Hanuman reduced his size to that of an ordinary monkey and alightened on a hill top.

37. Hanuman In Lanka

From his lofty position, Hanuman had a fine view of Lanka. He noted how well it was protected by thick walls. deep moats and impregnable fortresses.

"I have succeeded in the first part of my task and have crossed the ocean to reach Lanka. Now I must find out where Ravana had hidden Sita and if she is still alive!" Hanuman decided.

He knew that he would have to be very careful. For, if he made a mistake and was discovered, everything would be lost! So, he wisely planned to enter the city towards evening, just as darkness would fall.

Hanuman shrunk his size even more and became a very small monkey. He walked toward the city gates. Suddenly he was accosted by the guardian Goddess of the city.

"Who are you little monkey and what is your plan?"

"I am just a curious little monkey and have come to see this wonderful city!" Hanuman replied meekly.

The Goddess hit him. Hanuman returned the blow with his left hand. She fell to the ground and at once remembered an old prophecy that when a little monkey struck her down, the end of Ravana and the destruction of Lanka was at hand. But, she simply stood by and let Hanuman go. Her duty was to guard the entrance of the city and she was not Ravana's servant.

Hanuman felt that as he was entering the enemy's territory, he should not enter through the gates in the usual way. Instead, he jumped on the wall and leaped down to the ground on the other side. He walked along casually and, as he searched for Sita, his sharp eyes noted the strong defences of the city in case of enemy attack.

"What shall I do? Sita is nowhere to be found. How can I face the vaanaras who are depending on me to bring news of Sita's whereabouts... what shall I tell Rama, Lakshmana and Sugriva? Rama will surely die if Sita is not found! So, will Lakshmana! No! I must search more thouroughly!" Hanuman resolved.

He searched all over Ravanas palaces and the many buildings in Lanka, but there was no sign of Sita. He even entered Ravana's bed-chamber and looked at the ten-headed rakshasa with curiosity.

Then he remembered what Sampaati had said...that Sita was held captive in a beautiful garden. So, he decided to search in all the parks till he came to the Asoka Vana.

38. Sita In The Asoka Vana

The moment Hanuman entered the Asoka Vana, he felt a soothing sensation flowing through his entire body.

"This must be the place where Sita is! Let me climb up this tree to look all around!" he decided and climbed up an asoka tree.

Something made him look down. Seated under the spreading branches of the tree, Hanuman saw a divinely-beautiful woman. Her appearance was dishevelled, her hair uncombed and her face was stained with tears. She wore no jewels.

Hanuman felt a thrill of pleasure. He was sure that at last he had found Sita. She had thrown her jewels down when Ravana had carried her over the Rishyamooka hill, he remembered. Ugly rakshasis guarded the beautiful woman. Hanuman was filled with great pity but made up his mind to see what happened before he contacted her.

39. Ravana Warns Sita

As daylight dawned, there was the sound of royal fanfare which announced the arrival of the King of Lanka, Ravana. Hanuman concealed himself more effectively among the leaves in case he was spotted and watched Ravana walk up to Sita.

"O beautiful lady! Why do you shy away from me? Accept me and enjoy the wealth and position I lay at your feet! Why do you still pine for that Rama who has been exiled? You can take it from me that Rama can never cross the ocean and come to Lanka! he beseeched Sita.

Sita laughed with scorn and replied, "I was married to Rama and will accept no other man as my husband. How would you like it if another man cast a desiring look at your wife? Forget me, Ravana, and beg Rama's pardon. You are treading the path of doom and Rama will surely kill you!"

Ravana became furious. "How dare you speak so to the King of Lanka? I am becoming tired of your praising that worthless Rama! Remember, of the years' time I had given you to accept me, only two more months remain. If you still refuse to accept me, my cooks will cook you for my breakfast!"

Before he left the Asoka Vana, Ravana ordered the rakshasis guarding Sita to persuade her somehow.

The moment Ravana left, the rakshasis surrounded Sita.

"Come on, foolish one! The mighty Ravana desires you! Accept him and enjoy the wealth of Lanka!" one of them said.

"The great Ravana want you; but you turn your face away. Accept him and accept your good fortune!" added another rakshasi.

This went on for sometime. Sita wept uncontrollably, frightened by the ugly rakshasis' talk.

Just then, a rakshasi name Trijata, awoke and heard these words. She said, "Why do you all torment this saintly woman? They say that early morning dreams often come true. I just dreamed that our Lanka is in flames... that Rama will come soon and defeat Ravana!"

This scared the rakshasis who left Sita alone for the time.

40. Hanuman Gives Rama's Ring To Sita

Sita had never felt so desperate and lonely as she did now, and thought that she was suffering because she had unjustly accused the innocent Lakshmana. She wept bitterly and decided to end her life by hanging herself. Hanuman became furious with Ravana and the rakshasis for torturing Sita.

He was wise enough to know that Sita would naturally be suspicious of a stranger standing before her and think that it was a rakshasa in disguise.

He parted the leaves of the tree so that Sita could see him when looked up. Then in a soft voice which only she could hear, Hanuman sang the entire story of Rama...how he was the son of the great King Dasaratha of Ayodhya...how he was married to the princess Sita, daughter of King Janaka of Mithila...how Rama was exiled to the forest for fourteen years by his mother, Kaikeyi... how he had killed many rakshasas to help the sages...how Ravana had abducted his beloved wife Sita, by ordering Mareecha to appear as a golden deer before her... and how he was still searching for his kidnapped wife.

Hanuman paused awhile and then went on to describe how the grief-stricken Rama and Lakshmana had searched for Sita... how Rama had made friends with vaanara prince Sugriva and had killed Vali... how Sugriva had sent his vaanaras to search everywhere for Sita.

Sita looked all round to see who was singing such a beautiful song. No one was in sight so she looked up and saw a radiantly beautiful little monkey chanting the story of Rama.

Joy filled Sita's sore heart as Hanuman leaped down the tree and bowed to her.

"O Beautiful lady! Am I seeing Sita, the beloved wife of Sri Rama?" he asked. "Sri Rama has sent me here!"

"Are you really from Sri Rama?" Sita looked happy.

Hanuman eagerly took a step forward. Immediately Sita closed her eyes and moved away, thinking that Ravana had devised a new way to torture her.

So, Hanuman wisely moved back. From a safe distance, he repeated his song about Rama, and ended with the remark, "I am Rama's servant and can assure you that he will come soon to Lanka with Lakshmana to rescue you!"

As proof that Rama had indeed sent him, Hanuman bowed again and reverently handed over Rama's signet ring to Sita. This finally convinced Sita that Rama had sent Hanuman. She wept with joy as she told Hanuman to convey to Rama her wish that he should come within two months which had been given to her by Ravana or that she would end her life.

"O Mother! I cannot bear to see your grief! If you agree, I can carry you on my back across the ocean to Lord Rama!" Hanuman exclaimed as he saw Sita's tears.

He noted the doubt in her eyes about his strength to cross the ocean and began growing in size to show her the form in which he had crossed the ocean to come to Lanka.

"O son Hanuman! I believe that you are strong enough to carry me across the ocean. But I feel that it would not be correct - if rakshasas attacked you on the way back, you would feel handicapped by my presence on your back! No, the best way would be for Rama to come to Lanka, defeat Ravana in battle and rescue me like a true warrior and husband!" Sita said.

"Forgive me, Mother, you are right! I will go back at once and tell Lord Rama that I have seen you. Is there any token by which I can convince him that I really saw you and spoke to you?" Hanuman asked.

Sita took her choodamani or crown jewel and handed it to Hanuman.

"Rama will recognise this at once" she said.

Hanuman received the jewel, bowed to her and left the Asoka Vana.

41. Lanka On Fire

Hanuman took the form of an ordinary monkey as he sat on the garden wall. He thought that he should do something to put courage into Sita and at the same time scare Ravana so that he would not ill-treat Sita. So, he planned to attract attention to himself.

Hanuman began to grow in size and soon looked fearful in sight. He roared angrily and began to uproot the trees in the beautiful garden and laid waste the Asoka Vana, taking care not to touch the place where Sita sit.

The noise attracted the attention of the Rakshasis who reported to Ravana that a huge monkey had destroyed the beautiful Asoka Vana.

Ravana was furious and sent warriors to kill the monkey. He was even more angered when he learned that the monkey had killed them all.

So, he called his son, Indrajit, who had divine weapons, besides knowledge of black magic and told him to capture the monkey in the Asoka Vana.

Indrajit had once defeated Indra, the King of the Devas, in battle. He now lead a huge army of rakshasas to the Asoka Vana. After fighting with Hanuman and finding out that he could not be captured easily, Indrajit discharged the powerful Brahmastra. At once Hanuman lay bound and helpless.

Before Indrajit could do anything, the rakshasa soldiers ran forward and bound Hanuman with stout ropes from head to foot so that he could not move.

"Alas! The fools do not know that the divine Brahmastra loses its power the moment bonds of human nature like ropes comes in contact with it!" Indrajit thought to himself with dismay.

If Indrajit had obtained a boon from Brahma, so had Hanuman. Brahma had told him to submit to the Brahmastra meekly for a period of time after which it would lose its powers and he would be free. So, Hanuman lay submissively as the rakshasas dragged him through the streets of Lanka to Ravana's court. The common people mocked at Hanuman and laughed at him. He could have freed himself, but he did not do so. He wanted to further his role as Rama's messenger and warn Ravana and his rakshasas.

The rakshasa soldiers took Hanuman to Ravana's court where his ropes and chains were removed. He gazed at the majestic figure of rakshasa King Ravana with pity mixed with admiration. As he was not offered a seat, Hanuman lengthened his tail to form a high coil on which he sat and faced Ravana.

The ten-headed Ravana did not address Hanuman, directly, but asked his ministers to find out who he was and why he had come to Lanka.

"Our King wants to know who you are, monkey and why you have come here!" said Ravana's chief minister.

"My name is Hanuman. I am Sri Rama's messenger and have come to search for Sita who was kidnapped. O Ravana! You have abducted Sita, his wife. Return Sita at once to Rama and seek his pardon for acting in a manner contrary to dharma! Or, you and the rakshasa race will be destroyed by Rama, Lakshmana, Sugriva and his myriads of vaanara warriors!" Hanuman spoke boldly without a trace of fear.

Ravana's eyes turned red with anger.

"Put that impertinent monkey to death at once!" he shouted.

"No, brother! It would be wrong to kill a messenger who is just delivering a message!" Vibheeshana pointed out. "Just punish him and send him away!"

"All right! A monkey values his tail greatly. So, set fire to this animal's, beat him soundly and send him out!" Ravana ordered.

The rakshasa soldiers at once wound rags around Hanuman's tail which seemed to grow longer and longer! Then they poured oil on the rags and set fire to it. Hanuman was taken around the streets of Lanka, followed by a crowd of laughing rakshasas.

One rakshasa came running to the Asoka Vana and tauntingly informed Sita about Hanuman's tail being set on fire.

At once Sita prayed to Agni, the God of Fire, "O Agni Deva! Please stay cool to Hanuman and do not burn him with your heat!" Hanuman was deeply puzzled that though his tail was on flames, he did not feel the heat at all! He thought that perhaps Agni was being kind to him because of his friendship with his own father, Vaayu, the God of Winds.

Hanuman bore the insults quietly for some time. Then he felt that the time had come for him to teach the arrogant Ravana and his rakshasas a bitter lesson, which would be a foretaste of Rama's wrath.

Suddenly Hanuman contracted his form and shook off the ropes which bound him. He enlarged his shape once again and jumped from roof-top to roof-top of all the houses. They were set on fire by his burning tail and the wind fanned the flames so that the whole of Lanka began burning!

Hanuman looked at the scene with glee. He went to the sea and dipped his burning tail in the water to put out the fire. Then dismay filled him.

"Alas! What, if the Asoka Vana too has caught fire?! Sita is being held captive there!" he groaned.

To is utter astonishment he saw Sita sitting under the Asoka tree in the garden when he went there. He realised that it was Sita's purity which had saved him from the fire... which did not let the fire spread to Asoka Vana... which helped him to cross the vast ocean, for was it not all for Rama's sake?

"O Mother Sita! I am greatly relieved to see that you are safe and sound! It is all because of your immense power that no harm has come to you! Now please grant me leave to go - I shall tell Lord Rama all that has happened here!" He prostrated before Sita and accepted her blessings for the great journey ahead.

42. Hanuman's Happy Tidings To Rama

Hanuman lost no time in flying back across the ocean. He descended on the Mahendra mountain to the tumultuous welcome by Angada, Jambavan and the other vaanaras and narrated everything which had happened in Lanka.

"Let us go back and tell Sri Rama that Sita has been found!" Hanuman jubilantly led the monkey troop back to Kishkinda.

They reached a garden belonging to King Sugriva. The vaanaras ignored the protests of the park-keeper and ate all the fruits in the garden and drank the honey in the hives. The park-keeper complained to Sugriva who just smiled when he heard the news.

"Send the vaanaras here at once! They must have done this to celebrate good news" he said.

Sugriva's guess sounded like divine music to the ears of Rama and Lakshmana. They waited eagerly for the arrival of Hanuman, Angada, Jambavan and the other vaanaras who had gone south.

Angada and Jambavan urged Hanuman to relate once again all the events which had led to his meeting with Sita and also his meeting with Ravana.

Hanuman obeyed them and finally handed over the choodamani which Sita had sent. Rama recognised it at once and wept. He embraced Hanuman for his immense courage and wisdom, feeling sad that he could not reward him more richly. But Hanuman's entire body thrilled at Rama's touch which was precious to him!

"Let us all hasten to Lanka! Hanuman, you have told us that Ravana has given Sita two more months to give in!" Sugriva said.

Soon the huge army marched forward to the sea in the south.

"Let everyone rest after the long march. In the meanwhile, we shall decide how to cross the ocean to reach Lanka!" Rama said.

43. Rumblings In Lanka

Ravana was secretly disturbed. He had learned through his spies that a great army of vaanaras had reached the seashore on the opposite side. So, he summoned his ministers for a meeting.

They all tried to please the King and sang his praises. But there was one discordant note. It was struck by Vibheeshana, Ravana's younger brother. He spoke up fearlessly.

"O King! You may not like what I say, but I will say it and will be glad if you follow my advice! Please return Sita at once to Rama and seek his pardon. It was very wrong of you to kidnap another man's wife. But Rama will pardon you even now, before Lanka and our rakshasa race are destroyed" he said.

"Never! I will fight with my valiant rakshasas to the last!" Ravana replied.

Ravana then decided that they should all meet again the next day to discuss the matter.

Once more Vibheeshana spoke eloquently and tried to make Ravana see the error of his way.

"There have been bad omens in Lanka ever since you brought Sita here. Please return her to Rama!" Vibheeshana begged.

Ravana's face darkened with anger. "Never!" he shouted obstinately. "Never will I give up Sita!"

It was the turn of Kumbakarna, another brother of Ravana, to speak.

"O brother Ravana! you did commit a mistake by kidnapping Sita. But I am sure that we all can defeat Rama, Lakshmana and the vaanaras hordes. Why! I am ready to lay down my life for you!" he exclaimed.

Ravana felt encouraged to hear this and was happier when the other rakshasa warriors vowed to fight till the end.

Vibheeshana felt sad. He knew that he could not stay a moment longer in Lanka when Ravana would not relent and mend his ways. So, he told his brothers that he was leaving with a few of his trusted followers.

44. Vibheeshana Surrenders

Vibheeshana and four of his loyal companions rose in the sky and flew across the vast ocean. They saw the vaanaras camping on the seashore and remained suspended in the sky.

Sugriva recognised the form of the rakshasas and felt worried. He told the vaanaras to be prepared for anything which could happen.

Vibheeshana heard these words and began speaking calmly.

"O vaanaras! Do not worry. I am Vibheeshana, the younger brother of Ravana, King of Lanka. I begged him to return Sita to Rama and ask for forgiveness. But Ravana was angry with me. I decided to leave Lanka as it is impossible to stay there where there is no dharma. Now I stand before you all and seek Rama's forgiveness and grace! Please inform Rama of my intentions!"

Sugriva went to tell Rama about the new occurrence.

"I do not trust Vibheeshana. I am sure that it is trick of Ravana's to send his brother here, to find out what we have planned to do!" he said.

Many of the vaanaras agreed with Sugriva and did not wish to accept Vibheeshana. Rama then looked at Hanuman and asked him what he thought.

"O Lord Rama! Vibheeshana has come here openly seeking your protection as he disagrees with his brother about Sita's kidnapping. I feel that he is sincere and we should allow him to join us!" said Hanuman.

Rama was overjoyed to hear this.

"Whoever comes to me and seeks protection will not be rejected. Even if Ravana came for forgiveness I would not turn him away!" he stated.

Sugriva realised the truth of Rama's words and went to fetch Vibheeshana and his followers.

There, on the sandy seashore, Rama, Lakshmana and Sugriva, crowned Vibheeshana, King of Lanka.

45. Building The Bridge To Lanka

Now a new problem arose. How could the huge vaanara army cross the great ocean safely? Lakshmana, Sugriva and Vibheeshana discussed the matter. They advised Rama to pray to Varuna, the God of the Ocean, for help.

Rama agreed to pray to Varuna to make a passage way to Lanka for three days. Nothing happened. Rama became angry. He shot a powerful arrow into the water.

A radiant being emerged from the water. It was the God of the Ocean, Varuna. He stood before Rama with folded hands and said, "O Lord Rama! I cannot change my nature which is fast, deep and unconquerable to part the waters of the ocean and make a passage for you! But I will help you and will hold the bridge you construct. Every log and stone will bear the weight of your army safely! I can even tell you which place will be most suitable for a bridge!"

Rama understood and accepted Varuna's apology. Then the great work began. Under Varuna's guidance, Nala, the son of the great Viswakarma, built the bridge. The vaanaras enthusiastically brought mighty trees, huge boulders and rocks to the seashore.

Then the huge army crossed the ocean to Lanka.

46. Angada Is Sent As Messenger

Rama asked the vaanara warrior leaders to send Angada to him.

"O prince Angada! I want you to go to Ravana and convey a message from me! Listen to me..."

Accordingly, Angada went to Ravana's court.

"O Lord of Lanka! Rama has sent me with a message. I am Angada, son of the great Vali - surely you remember him! Rama has asked me to tell you that your hour of reckoning has come and that you will pay heavily for your kidnapping of his wife, Sita. If you wish, you can surrender and ask for forgiveness. Or, be prepared to meet him on the battlefield and lose everyone and everything in Lanka!" Angada said loudly.

Ravana's anger mounted. "Seize the vaanara and kill him!" he shouted.

A couple of rakshasas rushed up and caught hold of Angada, but he rose in the sky and flung the rakshasas down. Then he suddenly swooped down and kicked a tower of the palace. It broke and fell with a crash. Then, with a mighty leap, he returned to the place where Rama was waiting in the vaanara camp.

47. Ravana's Tactics

Ravana was deeply shaken by Angada's assault. He thought that the broken tower was a bad omen. He then sent spies to find out the strength of the enemy and what plans they had made.

The two rakshasas disguised themselves as vaanaras and mingled with the others. But Vibheeshana saw through their disguise and caught them. He led the two rakshasas to Rama. They said that Ravana had sent them and begged for mercy.

Rama allowed them to have a good look at his army and its defences. He told them to inform their King about all they had seen and that he should prepare for his death.

"O Lord! We still have a chance to survive death if Sita is returned to Rama!" one rakshasa dared to say in trembling tones to Ravana.

"No! Even if I lose the whole world, I shall not give up Sita!" Ravana shouted.

Then he followed a strange line of reasoning. He thought that Sita was resisting him because she knew that Rama was alive. If Rama was out of the way, Sita would give in to him, Ravana thought. So, he sent for a sorcerer.

"Conjure up a head which resembles that Rama!" he ordered.

The sorcerer did so at once, to Ravana's great delight.

"Stay here and come when ordered!" Ravana said and went to the Asoka Vana.

"O Sita! I have killed that husband of yours, Rama! So, lose no time in accepting me and enjoy the exalted position of Queen of Lanka!" he boasted.

"I do not believe you!" Sita replied bravely.

Ravana then ordered his rakshasa guard to fetch the person who was waiting outside the garden.

The person-really the sorcerer-came up and placed a blood-covered head and a sword dripping with blood, before Sita.

Sita cast a horrified look at the head and swooned at once. Just then a messenger came up and informed Ravana that his presence was required urgently by his ministers. So, Ravana left the Asoka Vana. At that very moment, Sita recovered consciousness and as soon as Ravana left, the head of Rama vanished in a puff of smoke.

Sita did not know to believe. A rakshasi, named Sarama, said, "O saintly lady! Fear not! Rama is not dead. It is nothing but a magic head made by Ravana, but his presence was necessary to keep up the illusion. The moment Ravana left, the head too vanished! I will tell you the truth - Rama has arrived in Lanka with huge vaanara army!"

Even as she spoke, the drums and bugles of warfare could be heard. Sita trembled with joy but the citizens of Lanka trembled with fear.

48. The War Begins

Rama had learned from Vibheeshana about the defences of Lanka. He now ordered the vaanara army to attack the rakshasas. A great battle began. Both sides were well-matched with brave warriors. Thousands of rakshasas were slain by the vaanaras who hurled huge boulders and giant trees to crush them. The battle raged throughout the day and at night, when the rakshasas, became stronger, they continued to fight.

Then Indrajit, well-versed in black magic, became invisible. He shot 'sarpa-astras'(serpent darts) at Rama and Lakshmana who fell down immobile. The vaanaras, led by Sugriva, Angada, Hanuman and Jambavan, felt helpless as they stared at the two princes of Ayodhya. Vibheeshana came up and saw what had happened.

"Do not grieve! Rama and Lakshmana will become all right soon! Just look, their faces look bright and their eyes are glowing. Some weapons has made them temporarily immobile!" he said encouragingly.

So, the vaanaras resumed fighting. But Ravana had the news about Rama and Lakshmana announced all over Lanka to hearten the rakshasas. He sent for some rakshasis and told them to inform Sita about the deaths of Rama and Lakshmana.

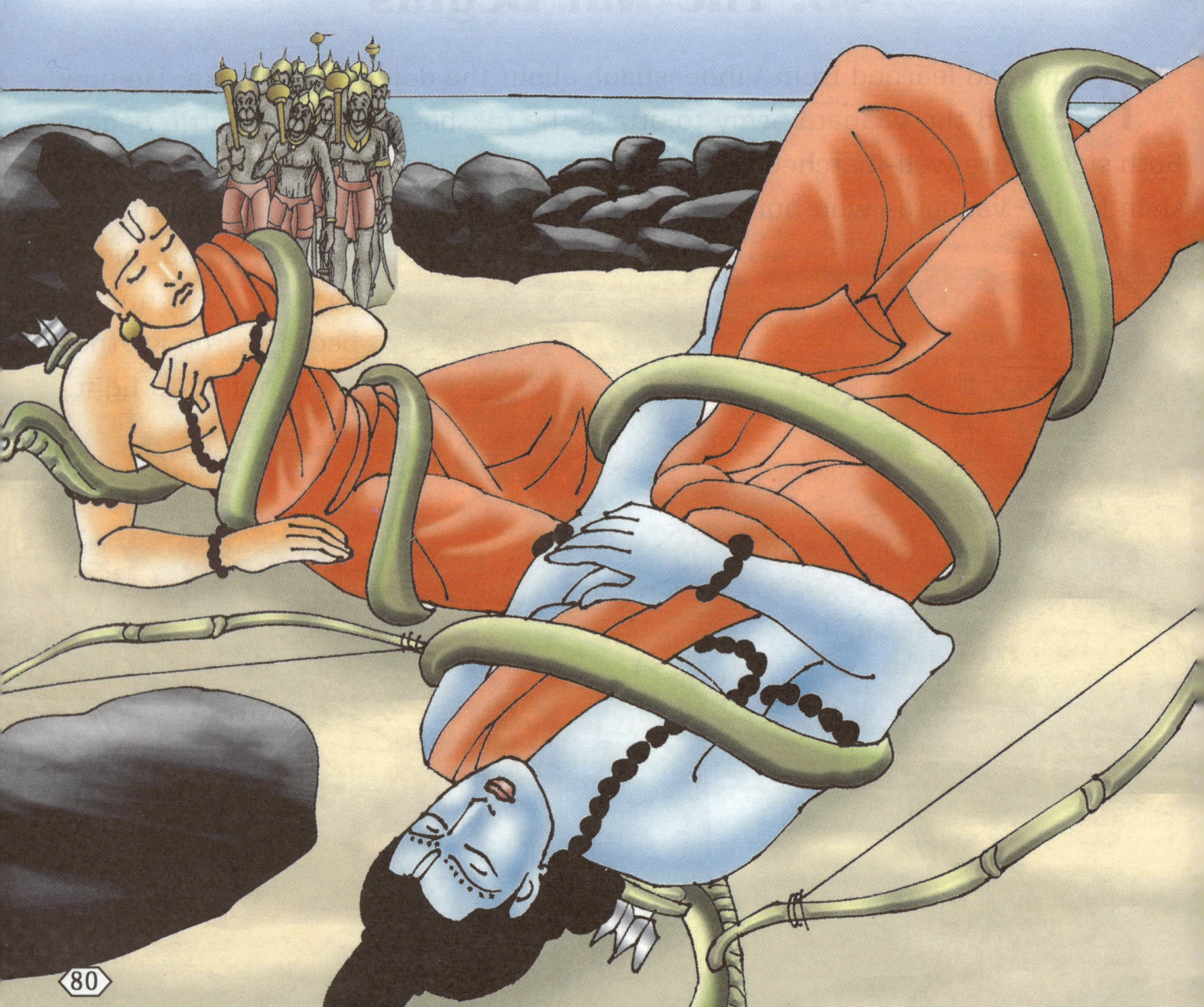

"Take her in the Pushpaka Vimana to see with her own eyes the two of them lying on the field!" he said.

As ordered, the rakshasis took Sita in the Pushpaka Vimana to the battlefield. Sita broke out into tears when she saw Rama and Lakshmana lying as if dead.

"Everything is over for me! What shall I do now?" she cried helplessly.

Trijata, the rakshasi who was kinder in her attitude to Sita then the rest, was present. She peered at Rama and Lakshmana closely and told Sita not to worry as the brothers were not dead, but stunned by some weapon. Sita returned to the Asoka Vana more comforted.

As the arrows powered by black magic weakened, Rama recovered gradually. But Lakshmana lay unmoving still. Rama wept when he saw his brother lying like one dead.

Then a wonderful thing happened. Huge waves rose in the sea and the winds blew alarmingly as a great bird circled down. It was Garuda, the mount of Vishnu.

The moment Garuda touched the ground, the serpents binding Rama and Lakshmana slithered away quickly. Garuda gently stroked the bodies of the two Ayodhya princes; so that they regained strength and sat up. The serpents in the magic weapons used by Indrajit, recognised their old foe, Garuda the eagle and departed.

The battle resumed with greater force than before.

49. Ravana Humbled

Ravana sent many more rakshasa warriors. They fought valiantly but were killed by Hanuman, Sugriva and Angada. So, he decided to go to the battlefield himself and rode in a great chariot. Rama saw the majestic ten-headed warrior and resolved to defeat him somehow.

But Ravana fought with great courage and killed many vaanaras. Seeing this, Sugriva was angry and came forward to attack the rakshasa. A great battle followed later between Ravana and Lakshmana, who fell down unconscious. Hanuman carried Lakshmana away on his shoulders.

Then Rama came to fight with Ravana. His arrows broke the rakshasa's chariot, killed the charioteer and also deprived him of all his weapons. Ravana stood helpless before Rama.

"You have fought well today! Go now and rest. We shall resume the battle tomorrow!" Rama told him.

Ravana shamefacedly retreated to his palace.

50. Kumbakarna Is Roused

Ravana smarted from this humiliation and vowed to defeat Rama somehow. "Kumbakarna has just begun his six-month long sleep. But I need his help urgently and must waken him up!" Ravana decided desperately.

Due to a curse, Kumbakarna slept for months and as Ravana had just said, Kumbakarna's sleep period had begun a few days ago. So, it would be a mammoth task to awaken the sleeping giant.

Ravana's ministers were aware that as soon as Kumbakarna was awakened, he would roar loudly for food. So, they ordered mountains of food and casks of drink to be prepared. Then they made a terrible uproar and even caused elephants to walk on him. Some rakshasas even beat him with stout sticks!

At last, Kumbakarna opened his eyes and yawned angrily. Before he found out why his sleep was disturbed, Kumbakarna first turned his attention to the vast quantities of food and drink spread before him.

When he had finished eating, Ravana's ministers told Kumbakarna that his presence was required urgently by Ravana.

"O brother Kumbakarna! That small man, Rama, has caused a bridge to be built across the ocean to Lanka and is now camping on the shore of our island with a huge vaanara army. The rakshasa warriors are vainly fighting them. But we have lost many brave warriors!" Ravana begun.

"O brother Ravana! You are responsible for this situation as you kidnapped Rama's wife. But do not worry, I shall go out at once, kill Rama and Lakshmana, and lay their heads at your feet!" Kumbakarna boasted.

He set forth with Ravana's blessings at the head of a huge army. His gigantic form presented a frightening sight to the vaanaras. Angada had to encourage them to fight and not flee.

Kumbakarna hit Hanuman with a lance, knocked him down. He then shot weapons at Sugriva who fell unconscious. Kumbakarna picked up the vaanara King and walked off with him. He wanted to show his prize catch to Ravana. As he strode down the street with the unconscious Sugriva on his shoulder, the citizens cheered and threw flowers and sandal paste on their hero. But the cool sandal paste revived Sugriva.

Sugriva realised where he was and tormented Kumbakarna by biting his nose and ears and scratching him with his long nails, so that the rakshasa let go of him. The moment he was free, Sugriva flew back to the battlefield followed by Kumbakarna.

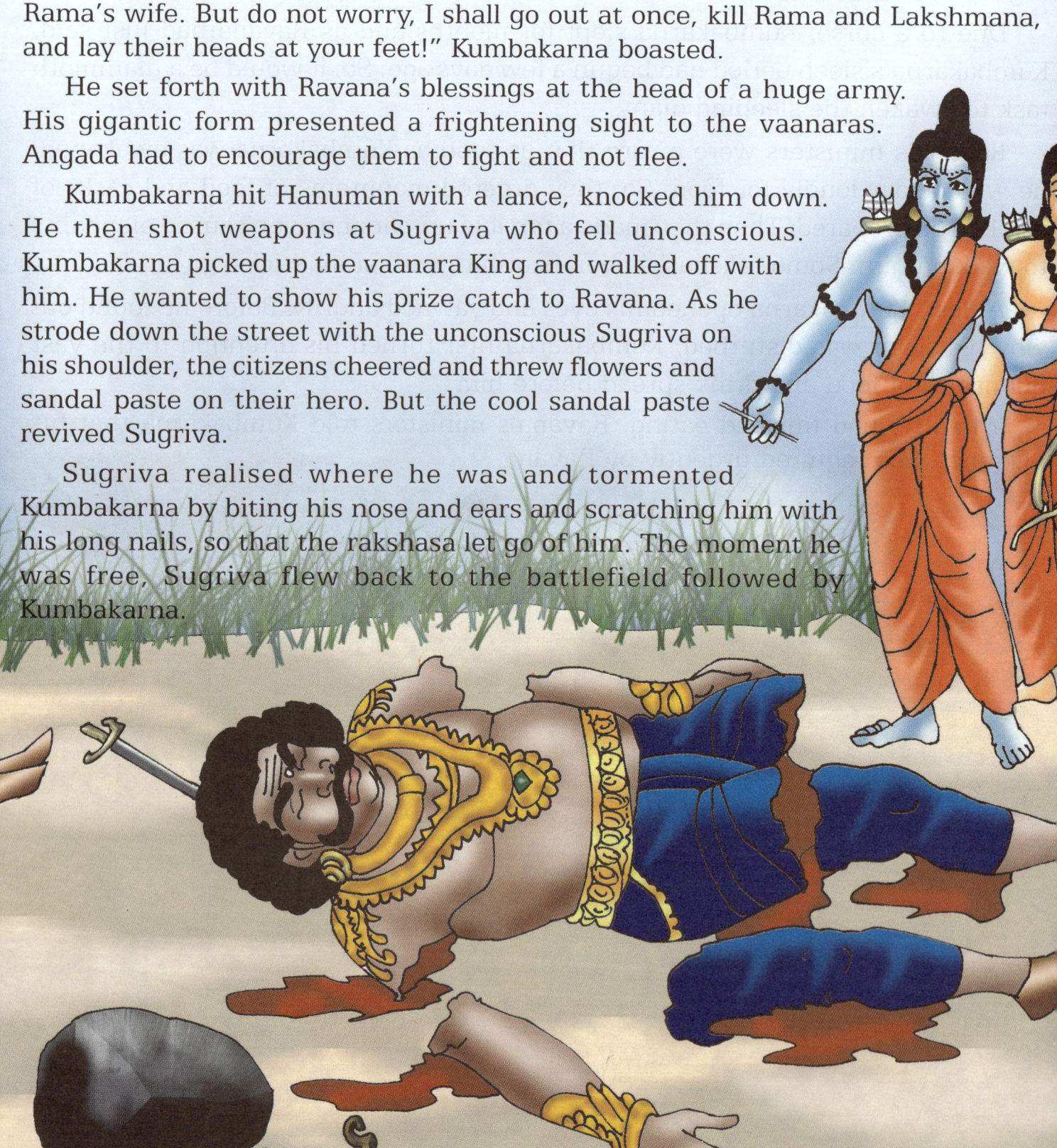

Now he looked even more hideous with his torn nose and ears. He fought ferociously and slaughtered the vaanaras. He ignored Lakshmana's advance and went straight to meet Rama.

Rama shot several powerful darts at Kumbakarna. But they did not deter the rakshasa. So, Rama used stronger weapons and cut off Kumbakarna's arms and feet. But the legless rakshasa still moved on his stumps to kill the vaanaras.

At last Rama shot an arrow which cut off Kumbakarna's head. The vaanaras rejoiced at the death of Kumbakarna. But Ravana was deeply grieved and shocked to hear this. His son, Indrajit, offered to go to the battlefield and kill Rama and Lakshmana.

Indrajit was a very brave warrior and knew the use of many weapons which he had obtained through penance. Above all, he was a master at black magic. He first fought in the usual way and soon resorted to invisibility as he shot arrows at the vaanaras from all sides. They were helpless against the invisible enemy.

Indrajit then aimed the Brahmastra at Rama and Lakshmana who feel down unconscious. He then went to report to Ravana about his feat.

The vaanaras were panic-stricken and thought that Rama and Lakshmana were dead. The aged vaanara, Jambavan, asked for Hanuman to be brought to him.

"O Hanuman, son of Vaayu! Go at once to the Himalayas in the north. The Hill of Herbs, the Sanjivini, is located there. Find four herbs which glow even in the dark and bring them here to revive Rama and Lakshmana" he said.

Hanuman rose in the sky and travelled with the speed of the wind to the Himalaya mountains. There, between the Rishaba and Kailasa peaks, he saw the Sanjivini Hill which had been described to him by Jambavan. But as he could not waste time, Hanuman lifted the entire hill and flew back to Lanka with it.

The approach of the Sanjivini Hill was enough to revive Rama and Lakshmana and all the vaanaras who were the spell of the Brahmastra. The herbs healed their wounds and gave them fresh strength.

Indrajit returned to the battlefield and saw that his effort had gone in vain. Once again he used black magic to fight with the vaanaras. With the help of this, Indrajit conjured up a maaya Sita and killed her in the sight of the vaanara army.

They rushed to inform Rama who fainted when he heard this. But Vibheeshana calmed Rama.

"Ravana will never allow Sita to be killed. It is just a trick by Indrajit to gain time to perform an asuric sacrifice of great power. If the sacrifice is performed, we can never defeat Indrajit. So, let Lakshmana, Hanuman and Sugriva to prevent the sacrifice from being completed. I will also go with them, for I know the temple, where Indrajit will be in!" he said.

The vaanara army went with Lakshmana, Hanuman, Sugriva and Vibheeshana to the temple where Indrajit was performing the sacrifice. He was forced to abandon it and begin fighting against Lakshmana. Lakshmana stood on Hanuman's shoulder and attacked Indrajit. The fight went on for quite some time. At last, Lakshmana shot the Indra-astra. He invoked the name of Rama and sent it forth. Indrajit's head was sliced from his body and fell to the ground. There was much cheering that dreadful foe had been killed.

51. The Death Of Ravana

Ravana was totally shattered by the death of his beloved son, Indrajit. "O my beloved son, Indrajit, before whom even the Devas trembled...are you gone from me forever? What shall I do now?" he cried. Soon his grief gave way to burning fury. "I shall go out at once and avenge your death!"

Ravana prepared for battle and armed himself with many weapons. Clad in armour, Ravana rode in his divine chariot to the battlefield. He brushed aside Lakshmana's opposition and faced Rama with courage.

All the Devas and Rishis gathered above to watch the greatest battle of all.

Both Rama and Ravana were excellent bowsmen. Both warriors had divine weapons. So, the contest between Rama and Ravana was long and equal; even the vaanaras and remaining rakshasas.

Rama found that his powerful arrow could not penetrate Ravana's armour. Rama cut off Ravana's ten heads one by one. But even one fell, another grow in its place.

Ravana laughed at Rama's puzzlement and was furious when Lakshmana and Vibheeshana attacked him. He hurled a powerful weapon at Vibheeshana which Lakshmana countered with an equally powerful dart. Once again Ravana attacked Vibheeshana who was a traitor in his eyes. Once again the weapon was countered by Lakshmana.

Ravana's eyes became red with burning fury. He hurled a mighty weapon at Lakshmana shouting "Now you are dead!"

Under its force, Lakshmana fell down unconscious.

Rama did not notice it, but continued fighting. Once again Hanuman brought an entire mountain of herbs to revive Lakshmana.

Indra, the King of Devas knew that Ravana's end was near. He told Maatali, his charioteer to take his divine chariot for Rama's last assault.

"My Lord, Indra has sent his chariot for you to use!" Maatali said to Rama.

Rama bowed to the King of the Devas, climbed the chariot. Then began a great battle eagerly watched by the Devas, Gandharvas and rishis.

"O Lord Rama! May I remind you of the Brahmastra?!" Maatali whispered to Rama.

Then Rama invoked Brahma and hurled the Brahmastra. It pierced Ravana's chest and he fell down dead.

"At last Ravana is dead. Glory to Rama for destroying the wicked rakshasa race!" - the Devas, Gandharvas and rishis cried and showered flowers from above at Rama.

On the battlefield, however, everyone was quite stunned by the sudden end of Ravana. There was great mourning in Lanka. Ravana's wives, led by the beautiful Mandodari, wept at the side of the slain rakshasa.

52. Sita's Ordeal By Fire

Vibheeshana too grieved over the death of his brother.

"O Vibheeshana! Do not be so sad! Ravana died like a true warrior, on the battlefield. And death has washed away his many sins. Arise and perform his last rites!" Rama said.

Soon Vibheeshana was properly crowned King of Lanka. Rama then asked Hanuman to go with the King's permission to the Asoka Vana and convey all the happenings to Sita.

Hanuman accepted Vibheeshana's permission and reported to Sita in the Asoka Vana. She, in her reply, said that she was eager to meet Rama.

When Hanuman conveyed Sita's message to Rama, he was sent back to inform Sita that Rama wished her to come to him freshly-bathed and bedecked with jewels. This time Vibheeshana went with Hanuman. When Sita said that she would go as she was, Vibheeshana told her about Rama's wish and ordered the women to adorn Sita with jewels befitting a Queen. Then she was taken in a palanquin to Rama. All the vaanaras pressed forward to catch a glimpse of Sita. So, she alighted from the palanquin and walked to the palace where Rama was standing to allow everyone to see her.

At last Sita was face to face with her husband, Rama. Tears of happiness streamed from her eyes. But Rama seemed to be lost in thought. After some time he said, "Now I have done my duty like a true Kshatriya and killed Ravana who kidnapped you. But how can I take you back as you have lived for a year in a stranger's - my enemy's - dwelling?! So, we cannot live together any more!"

Sita was utterly shocked and distressed by Rama's words.

"My heart has been broken by your cruel words. Remember, I come from a great family! It is not my fault that I was kidnapped by a rakshasa! As you doubt

me, there is only one course left for me to follow!"

She turned to Lakshmana who too seemed to angry with his brother, and asked him to light a big fire.

Sita went round her husband and approached the blazing fire with folded hands. "O Agnideva! If I am pure and chaste, protect me!" she cried and jumped into the fire.

Everyone present was horrified.

Then Agnideva himself rose from the flames and lifted Sita totally unharmed. He presented her to Rama.

Rama accepted Sita joyfully and said, "I knew all the time about your purity, O Sita! But I had to do this, make you undergo the ordeal by fire for the sake of the world!"

53. Rama Meets Bharata

Now, Rama and Sita were truly united. Together with Lakshmana, Sugriva and Vibheeshana they ascended the Pushpaka vimana and flew back to Ayodhya. Hanuman flew in advance to tell Bharata that Rama was returning to Ayodhya after the fourteen years long exile.

As they flew back, Rama pointed out to Sita, the great bridge to Lanka which the vaanaras had built...the Rishyamooka hill where he had met Hanuman and had befriended the fugitive vaanara prince...the Kingdom of Kishkinda...the place where he and Lakshmana had last seen Jataayu. They reached sage Bharadwaja's ashrama and sought his blessings.

"Look, Sita, the good Guha and Bharata have both come to meet us!" Rama embraced Bharata and Guha.

Ayodhya was a sea of happiness. The people celebrated for many days as their beloved Rama had returned safely from his exile. Now Rama was crowned King at a magnificent ceremony witnessed by Hanuman, Sugriva, Vibheeshana and his countless well-wishers.

Rama's rule, known as RAMA RAJYA, was a time of peace, prosperity and plenty for the people of Ayodhya.

!!! SRI RAMAJAYAM !!!